Gardens of Genius

HAMLYN

London·New York·Sydney·Toronto

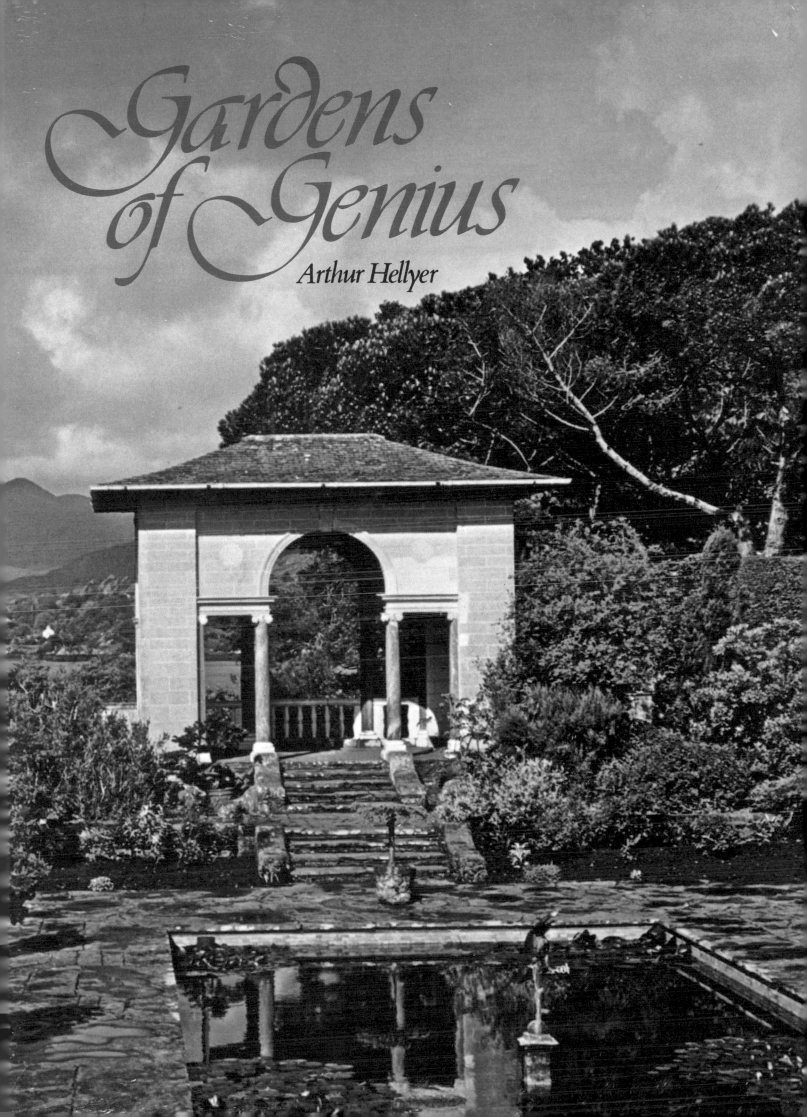

Gardens
of Genius

Arthur Hellyer

ACKNOWLEDGEMENTS

Photographs
John Bethell, St Albans 67, 118–119; Pat Brindley, Cheltenham 162, 163 left; Peter Burton, Scarborough 26; J. Allan Cash, London 22; Country Life, London 12, 21, 24, 25, 28, 29, 37, 41, 56, 69, 72, 77, 92, 96, 101, 105, 116, 129, 133, 136, 153, 156, 160, 168, 176, 185, 188, 201, 204, 205, 209, 210; Derbyshire Countryside Ltd., Derby 182–183; Hamlyn Group Picture Library 16, 20, 181 bottom; Iris Hardwick Library of Photographs, Cerne Abbas 39, 111, 130–131, 134–135, 138, 163 right; Arthur Hellyer, Crawley 11, 15, 31, 38, 43, 44, 46, 47, 49, 50 left, 50 right, 54, 55 right, 59, 61, 62, 63, 64, 75, 78, 80, 90, 95, 98–99, 103, 113, 114, 124, 127, 146, 154, 158, 174, 175, 178, 180, 187, 193, 194–195, 195, 213, 214, 215; Jarrold Colour Publications, Norwich 42, 55 left, 166–167, 179, 202, 203; Mansell Collection, London 144 top, 181 top; National Trust, London 34, 82, 83, 84, 141, 147, 148; National Trust for Scotland, Edinburgh 8, 51, 173; Sheila J. Orme, Chiddingford 33, 89, 91, 121, 144 bottom, 159, 197; Harry Smith Horticultural Photographic Collection, Chelmsford 10, 14, 35, 70, 71, 79, 86, 87, 106–107, 107, 123, 139, 150, 151, 170, 171, 190, 207; R. F. Thompson, London 74–75; Derek Tilley, Chesham 164; Jeremy Whitaker, Headley 18–19, 27, 30, 115, 122, 142, 143, 198–199.

Line work by David Bryant

Map by Eye Graphics

First published in 1980 by
The Hamlyn Publishing Group Limited
London·New York·Sydney·Toronto
Astronaut House, Feltham, Middlesex

Filmset in England by Servis Filmsetting Limited
in 12 on 14pt. Bembo
Printed and bound in Spain
ISBN 600 34086 4

Contents

Introduction

Everyone agrees that British gardens are rather special. Visitors come from all over the world to see them, and for the British public garden visiting has become a major relaxation. Well over 2,000 gardens are open to the public at some time every year. Charities such as the National Trust, The Queen's Institute of District Nursing, The Gardeners' Royal Benevolent Society and the Royal Gardeners' Orphan Fund have benefited greatly from all this enthusiasm.

What is by no means so clear is what it is that people regard as being the special quality of British gardens, nor even whether any clear consensus of opinion on such a matter exists. To me it appears that what the historians and the professional experts regard as most important is markedly different from what the public prefers. I often wonder which view future generations will take when they look back at our era.

We started garden making rather late by comparison with some other European countries and showed little originality during the first hundred years or so. We were content to take most of our ideas from the Italians, French and Dutch. But when, in the early 18th century, we did at last set off on a course of our own we exhibited quite unexpected inventiveness and before the century was out we were being widely copied as far afield as North America and Russia. *Le Jardin Anglais* became the mode though often the interpretation given to British ideas (perhaps at this stage one should say 'English', for the style did not receive much encouragement in Scotland, Wales or Ireland) was highly idiosyncratic.

It is the landscape style which the experts regard as the highest achievement of our garden making, some would say of our whole artistic output. They rave about it, write voluminous books on the subject and constantly regret that we no longer produce anything so good. Yet, with the solitary exception of Stourhead which some of the professionals would say has been spoiled by modern planting, it is not the great 18th century landscapes that attract the garden loving public nor, I think, is this the kind of garden that most visitors from overseas visualise when they speak of the British (or maybe English) style.

What they enjoy is something totally different. It is the far more cosy, inward-looking gardens of our own century; gardens which have been conceived as environments for people and plants and which are full of flowers and foliage for much of the year. In fact it was the gradually dawning realisation by the highly-experimental gardeners of the 19th century that the British climate and geology were uniquely favourable for plants that produced the second great revolution in our garden making and, arguably, the one that has most spread our fame abroad.

Yet this kind of flowery garden has been almost entirely the concern of amateurs and has earned little approval from the top professional designers, most of whom regard it as sentimental and disorganised. Perhaps this is just another example of the ever widening gap between experts and the general public in all the arts. However, even if this is so it does not follow that the professionals are right and the amateurs are wrong.

Garden making with plants is never completed since the plants grow out of scale, or become aged and die, and so are in constant need of control and renewal. To preserve such gardens at their peak requires meticulous supervision, a considerable knowledge of plants and a clear understanding of the effects that are required and the way in which they can be produced. Clearly these are tasks at which the garden owner, who is there all the time, is at a considerable advantage over the professional adviser, who appears only occasionally on the scene.

It is the purpose of this book to draw attention, in greater detail than is possible in the usual brief guide book, to some of the gardens which seem to me especially to express the British genius for garden making. Because I believe that the genius of our own times is at least as vivid as that of the past, it contains many gardens that have been created or considerably altered during this century. I hope readers will consider that I have included sufficient examples from the more distant past to present a fair picture of our highly versatile genius for garden making.

Arthur Hellyer

The Pattern Makers

*I*t took a long time for England to draw out of the middle ages. The conflict between king and barons continued for centuries and even when it was at last resolved, turmoil continued and most men of wealth found it necessary to live within fortifications. But as the power of the throne increased and law and order began to be enforced more evenly and certainly, even in distant parts of the country, a more gracious style of living began to assert itself and elegant mansions superseded castles. What has always astonished me is the speed and apparent ease with which the change was made. No sooner, it would seem, had castle making ceased than some of the most beautiful houses ever to be built in Britain were being erected. One of the loveliest of them all is Montacute House near Yeovil in Somerset built for an ambitious lawyer, Edward Phelps, from 1588 onwards. So far as I know the architect and builder, probably one and the same person, is unknown, yet his skill was clearly consummate. Had he travelled to Italy and seen, first hand, the great buildings of the Renaissance or was he merely following instructions and hearsay? I have no idea, but there must have been large numbers of other builders in many parts of the country making similar buildings, though not many with quite the flights of fantasy which make Montacute House so outstandingly lovely.

Gardens took a little longer to get off the mark though, when it did become the fashion, it was to Italy and France that the garden makers turned for inspiration. It was order and symmetry that they sought and found in good measure, together with all manner of embellishments for those who could afford them. Terraces were level, paths mainly straight, parterres and their attendant knots as simple or elaborate as taste and pocket might dictate. Masonry figured largely in these early gardens in which walls, balustrades, flights of steps and paths, flagged or gravelled, delineated the main outlines of the garden, at any rate in the vicinity of the house. Further afield there might be woodland but even this would most likely be intersected by wide rides and narrower allées formed with trees or bushes clipped to keep the shapes clean and clear and to sustain the message that, here, at least, man was in complete command of his surroundings. Pattern was the order of the day and evergreen shrubs, such as box, yew and phillyrea, which would submit to frequent trimming, were much in demand to fill in the details of the designs and provide it with striking focal points or oft repeated accents. Since a pattern made on the ground can be best seen from above, the best parterres were planted close to buildings where they could be viewed from the windows or they might be flanked or surrounded by raised walks from which they could be seen to advantage.

Another popular device was the mount, an artificial hill sometimes made in the centre of a garden, sometimes at its perimeter. There might be a pavilion or arbour of some kind on top and a serpentine path by which the mount could be ascended without too much effort. Its purpose was twofold, to provide a vantage point from which the pattern and good order of the garden could be admired and a lookout from which the outer world could be viewed without venturing outside the protective garden boundary. For though, by this time, the countryside was much safer and more settled than it had been, all was not yet completely secure and the walled garden was a haven of safety as well as a delight.

There are no plans or records to reveal what the first garden at Montacute House was like or even whether it had a garden at all. The twin gazebos, or two-storey pavilions, which are the corner pieces of the courtyard, seem perfectly designed for looking down in comfort and safety at such a garden as I have just

Two of the elaborately patterned beds on the parterre at Pitmedden House

9

described but in fact the records show that when it was first built this courtyard was the main entrance to the mansion and that the drive came from the east and not from the west as it does today. This would imply that the courtyard was mainly paved and that anyone sitting in either of the gazebos would have been watching the coming and going of coaches, carts and horsemen rather than gardeners trimming the evergreen knots and tending the flowers. What is certain is that the garden at Montacute House today, which seems to fit the property so well, is in fact partly the creation of Mrs Ellen Phelps and her skilful gardener Mr Pridham, starting about 1834 and continuing well into Queen Victoria's reign, and partly of Vita Sackville West and Mrs F.E. Reiss working for the National Trust after that invaluable organisation took over Montacute in 1931. Inside the building two large tapestries hang on the walls depicting gardens of the formal type that might have embellished Montacute House in its early days, but they come from Stoke Edith and have no connection with Montacute.

Most of the early formal gardens have disappeared, some swept away needlessly during the 18th-century landscape revolution, some dismantled or abandoned in the 20th century as the cost of maintaining them became insupportable. Yet thankfully a few remain and there have been some faithful reproductions made by owners with a sense of history or a preference for the disciplined designs of 17th-century garden makers rather than the more emotional and individualistic experiments of succeeding ages.

Edzell Castle and Pitmedden

The walled garden of Edzell Castle at Edzell, north of Brechin in Tayside, may well be the oldest complete garden design remaining in Britain and it is certainly one of the most charming. Yet it remains little known, possibly because it is now maintained by the office of the Secretary of State for Scotland which does not engage in a great deal of publicity. Moreover, Edzell lies a little off the main tourist routes, though it is easy enough to reach from the main road from Forfar to Aberdeen, and the journey can be continued over the beautiful Howe of the Mearns to rejoin the same road or alternatively to make the descent through Glen Dye to Banchory.

Edzell Castle is a small castle built early in the 16th century to which a modest mansion was added by Sir David Lindsay later in the century. Sir David was obviously a man of learning and good taste, who is known to have travelled widely. He had no doubt seen many of the great Continental gardens of the period. What he planned for his Scottish home was something on a far more intimate scale, but with a degree of sophisticated decoration that must have been very unusual in Scotland at that date.

The visitor approaches Edzell Castle from the back, and the garden is completely concealed from view. All he is aware of is a pleasant ruin of

Opposite: Part of the parterre at Pitmedden House

Right: The early 17th-century garden and garden house at Edzell Castle

lovely rose-coloured stone seen over a high wall of the same material. It may strike him even from the outside that this wall is of unusually interesting design, the heavy coping broken by a succession of slightly raised and carved pediments which give it the appearance of an ornamented battlement. Near the point at which the wall joins the main building is a narrow gateway, bearing the date 1604, which gives access to the garden. What meets the visitor within, unless he has been forewarned, is a complete and delightful surprise.

The garden is a rectangle, approximately 170 feet long and 140 feet wide, enclosed on three sides by the wall and on the fourth by the dwelling. The wall is now revealed as elaborately carved and recessed, the series of pediments surmounting it being the capstones of little box-like structures designed to contain niches facing inwards. Originally, no doubt, each niche contained a statue or bust, though these have long since disappeared. The walls are divided into panels of two sizes, once defined by pilasters, though these too have now gone. The smaller panels are still filled by fine stone carvings and the larger ones are recessed in a chequerboard pattern. There are 21 carvings in all, seven on each wall, those on the east side representing the planetary deities of Saturn, Jupiter, Mars, Sol, Venus, Mercury and Luna. Those on the south wall represent the liberal arts: grammatica, rhetorica, dialectica, arithmetica, musica and geometrica. On the western side, the cardinal virtues – faith, hope, charity, prudence, temperance, fortitude and justice – are represented.

Below each carving is a large recess for flowers, and each of the smaller dished recesses in the large panels is also filled with flowers. It is believed that these recesses were originally painted blue and filled with white flowers, thus with the red of the stone completing the gules, argent and azure of the Lindsay coat of arms. Today they are unpainted but filled alternately with growing plants of purple lobelia and white alyssum while

the larger recesses below the carvings are filled with orange and yellow marigolds. An anachronism, perhaps, since none of these would have been available to Sir David Lindsay. They are so entirely charming, however, as to disarm all criticism.

The heavy, sloping coping stones project a little, like a roof, and beneath their shelter the wall has been pierced at intervals to allow birds access to the space within, so that they may nest there. It is just one more of the delightful touches that makes the garden so unique. Originally, buildings stood at both corners of the garden removed from the house: to the east, a two-storey garden house which still stands in excellent condition; to the west, a bath house and well, of which little more than the foundations remain.

When HM Office of Works took over the care of this property between 1932 and 1935 the buildings and walls were much as we see them today, but all trace of the original garden within had disappeared. This, therefore, had to be reconstructed. It has been done in the style of a parterre, the eight beds of which are arranged around an octagon in the centre, the whole contained by a low box hedge and accented with cones and broad pillars of yew. The designs for the knots have been taken from some of the decorative stonework on the walls and include the fleur-de-lys, shamrock, rose and thistle as well as the motto of the Lindsays: *Dum spiro spero.*

Nothing is known of those whom Sir David Lindsay employed in the construction of his garden. That he was his own designer and employed local labour seems almost certain, and there is some evidence that three masons may have been employed since there is a slight difference in the quality of the carvings on each of the three walls. The panels themselves were copied from a 16th-century German book of engravings and the initials of the engraver have been included in the sculpture depicting Mars. Perhaps the mason, so skilled in his craft, was yet sufficiently naive to believe that these initials formed part of the design.

Another 17th-century garden that retains a lot of its original character is at Pitmedden House, Pitmedden, Grampian. The parterre here is six times the size of that at Edzell Castle. Work did not start on it until more than half a century later, but it lacks the sophisticated charm of its predecessor and has suffered more by change of use and dereliction. At Edzell, the pattern was always largely a vertical one, created by the elaborate walls, with the parterre which they enclosed being of secondary importance. At Pitmedden, it was quite otherwise, the pattern being mainly horizontal and three of the massive grey stone walls being required primarily to retain the high terraces from which it could be viewed almost in plan. Architectural ornament is much less important than at Edzell Castle, though the descent from the house terrace to the parterre is by way of a handsome divided stairway with stone balustrades and pillars at the top and two matching stone pavilions are placed one in each corner of the main terrace wall.

However, this must always have been subsidiary to the elaborately-patterned beds in the three-acre parterre below, and these, like those of Edzell Castle, have had to be entirely reconstructed. No record remained of what they may have looked like when originally planned by Sir

The wall at Edzell Castle with niches for flowering plants and perforations for bees and birds

Alexander Seton some time in the latter half of the 17th century. Therefore, when the property was presented by Maj. James Keith to the
National Trust for Scotland in 1952, it was necessary to draw up entirely
new plans fot it. Sir Alexander Seton does not appear to have travelled so
extensively as Sir David Lindsay, but, as Scottish Lord of Justiciary and the
representative for the County of Aberdeen in the Scottish Parliament he
must have been aware of all current trends of opinion and fashion. For his
own garden he may well have consulted Sir William Bruce, then engaged
on new work at the Palace of Holyrood House. That, at least, has been the
assumption of the Trust's advisers, who have therefore prepared designs
for four new patterns, three based on those known to have been used at
Holyrood, the fourth in the same idom but incorporating the coat of arms
and motto of Sir Alexander Seton. All this has been carried out with great
skill, the elaborate designs clearly defined by miles of trim box edging
accented with yews, and the whole given, as a suitably impressive centrepiece, a handsome fountain and basin partly formed of fragments of an
original Pitmedden fountain, partly of stones from a contemporary
fountain at Linlithgow, all apparently the work of Robert Milne, the
King's master mason. To attract visitors, who must flock to Pitmedden if
the garden is to pay its way, it has been thought necessary to colour this
pattern with the gayest annuals, 30,000 of which are raised each year in
nearby glasshouses. The result is undeniably effective and might well have
delighted Sir Alexander had he been familiar with any one of the exotic
plants included, which seems highly improbable.

*Modern planting in an
historic garden at Pitmedden
House*

*Avenues intersect at a stone
urn at Bramham Park*

Bramham Park

One of the most complete early gardens in England is at Bramham Park, West Yorkshire about a mile west of the A1 road. Except that it is also geometric in design, there is little similarity between this garden and the enclosed parterres of Edzell Castle and Pitmedden House.

Robert Benson, who became the first Lord Bingley, got his ideas for Bramham Park from the great formal gardens of le Nôtre in France and from Italy. What he set out to create was a series of impressive vistas, some of great length, framed in clipped trees and evergreen hedges with infilling of other trees and shrubs to give that dense, woodland appearance that the French call 'boscage'. The pattern of avenues and allées is fairly complex with six straight walks forming a rectangular grid based on the house and four others running transversely across these. There are two large water features though, rather surprisingly, neither is placed in the main axis from the house as it almost certainly would have been in a French garden of the period. Indeed at Bramham the house itself has no avenue centred on it and is faced by a large formal rose garden recessed into the land which at this point slopes upwards from the house.

The largest water feature is a double canal, always referred to as the T canal because one arm crosses the top of the other arm but not at right angles as one might expect. This slightly odd form was presumably adopted because, though the canal was placed well off centre from the house its large arm, the downstroke of the T, was to be directed towards it. Presumably the intention was to catch the reflection of the building in the water as the long canal does so effectively at Vaux-le-Vicomte. However it does not appear that Robert Benson employed any professional designer, certainly not one with Le Nôtre's natural genius for optics, and so his T canal only reflects the top storey of Bramham House and that is not very impressive. The shorter cross canal fares better being centred on one of the long alleys with a fine urn on a pedestal at its far end to act as an eye catcher.

There are other ornaments at intersections of the allées but the most effective eye catcher of all is an obelisk a long way to the south centred on the Broad Walk which passes in front of the house, separating it from the rose garden. Seen from this point the distant obelisk seems to stand in the garden giving the impression that this is of vast size. In fact to reach it one must cross a farm field, climbing a fence and ascending a ha-ha on the way, but the journey is worth while for it leads to the discovery of a fine domed temple beyond the obelisk. Again it seems strange that so conspicuous and expensive an ornament should have been placed where it makes so little contribution to the design considered as a whole.

There is the same element of amateurishness about the elaborate set of pools which are at the obelisk end of the Broad Walk for there again, because of the contours of the land, they are invisible from the house and do not really compose with any other part of the garden. A gothic temple stands on higher ground to the west but yet again the design falters and one is left with few effective vistas to portray in pictures.

Yet Bramham Park has charm and dignity and is now gaining horticultural interest by the addition of many exotic shrubs grouped informally in the modern manner but placed where they do not interfere with the original formal conception of Robert Benson.

Bramham Park suffered a terrible disaster during one night in February 1962 when a freak gale blew down over 200 of the largest trees, mainly beeches, some of them 250 years old, which framed the vistas. For a time it seemed that, as an example of the 17th-century style of gardening, Bramham was finished. However, thanks to the energy and vision of the owner and generous help from public funds, all the avenues and allées

Bramham Park after the disastrous gales of 1962

have been replanted. Some are already restored to something like their previous beauty and in others one can get a clearer idea of how this garden, and others of its kind, must have appeared during the lifetimes of their creators.

Powis Castle

Lead figure of a shepherd at Powis Castle

Because Italy is such a mountainous country, with the Apennines running down the country like an enormous spine and the Alps closing it in to the north, a great many Italian gardens are made on steeply sloping sites. It is not surprising, therefore, that Italian garden makers became adept in manipulating elevation to enhance their designs. During the Renaissance their deep terraces and superb stairways soon became famous and attracted many imitations. However in Britain hillside gardens are much less common and there are not many surviving examples that could be described as truly Italian in inspiration. The magnificent cascade at Chatsworth remains virtually untouched by time though the garden around it is very different from what it was when this vast water stairway, issuing from an elaborate stone building was constructed in the late 17th century. It could fairly be described as Italian in manner though it was actually made for the 1st Duke of Devonshire by Grillet, who had learned his art from Le Nôtre. A similar formal cascade at Dyrham, designed and built by London and Wise at about the same time, was swept away long ago in the cause of economy.

Only at Powis Castle, just inside Wales at Welshpool, can one see a complete garden of this period made on a steep escarpment quite clearly from Italian models. It must always have been one of the finest of its type and it is gratifying that it has been so little altered and so well maintained.

The land falls so steeply below the east face of this lovely pink sandstone castle that, to make a garden at all, it was necessary to construct a number of deep terraces retained by brick walls. There are four in all and below them a steep grassed slope terminated now by a large level area of plain grass where originally there was a water parterre presumably as formal and patterned as the terraces themselves. It is the only important part of the whole design that has disappeared completely.

According to the guide books this remarkable garden was made by the Earl of Rochford during the reign of William and Mary. No professional architect or builder is named and it may be that the earl was, in fact, his own designer though he must surely have employed a skilful mason to guide him on the details of construction. For the terraces are elaborate and ingenious, each differing from all the others in depth, width and design yet all linking together to make a harmonious and impressive composition. This is best viewed from the tongue of hillside which sweeps around the parterre to south and east. During the last century this has been converted into a well stocked woodland garden with many exotic trees and shrubs, including rhododendrons and azaleas, and it provides a pleasant contrast to the formality of the terraces without in the least interfering with them.

Lead statues on the second terrace at Powis Castle

The top terrace is the narrowest and plainest though its back wall is ornamental with tall, pedimented niches each containing a bust on a pillar. Steps lead down to the second terrace which has a stone balustrade the central portion of which curves and bears delightful lead figures of shepherds and shepherdesses. Brick arches at the back of this terrace give access to an arcade built beneath the top terrace and presumably once used as an aviary for traditionally this is known as the aviary terrace.

A similar device has been used on the third, or main, terrace, but here the area excavated beneath the terrace above is even larger and its front is glazed with deep sash windows. It was clearly built as an orangery. From one end of this terrace a path winds steeply downhill to the level floor of the valley and what was once the kitchen garden. This still retains some fruit trees though their role is now ornamental rather than utilitarian. The path descends between massive hedges of box and above these are even larger hedges of yew which match the large cones of yew beneath the walls of the castle itself. All contribute to a single purpose, to create a vast vertical pattern, sculptural in its three-dimensional solidity and entirely satisfying as a setting for an exceptionally beautiful castle. From all the terraces there are delightful views across the Vale of Powis to the Long Mountain which encloses it to the east.

Powis Castle now belongs to the National Trust and its gardeners have made excellent use of the warmth and charm of the terraces to establish on them a considerable collection of perennial plants both shrubby and herbaceous. They cost far less in time, labour and money to maintain than conventional bedding plants and are far more interesting for garden loving visitors. Since no one knows precisely what was grown on these terraces originally and most illustrations suggest that planting of that period would not seem very attractive to modern eyes it seems sensible to use good plants suitable for the site and arranged in the most effective way possible so long as this can be done without detriment to the overall design.

There is, in any event, change which is inevitable in all gardening. In the Earl of Rochford's time none of the topiary specimens could have grown to anything like the size they are today. No doubt he saw them as relatively small embellishments on his grand design. Today they tend to dominate it giving it a romantic appearance very different from the neat formality he intended.

Opposite: The Japanese garden at Tully House

An engraving of Powis Castle in 1742

Yet no one in their senses would suggest that they should now be replaced with small clipped yews and low box hedges. Powis Castle is appreciated for what it has become and imagination must be used to picture it as it once was.

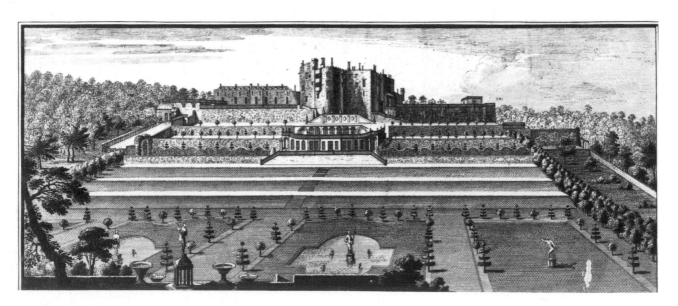

The
Picture
Makers

he idea that gardens need not invariably be made to formal patterns had begun to dawn on Englishmen well before the close of the 17th century. As early as 1685 Sir William Temple in his book 'Upon the Gardens of Epicurus' published in 1885, the year that Charles II died and James II succeeded him, was noting that the Chinese had a totally different outlook. 'Among us', he wrote, 'the beauty of building and planting is placed chiefly in some certain proportions, symmetries or uniformities; our walks and trees ranged so as to answer one another, and at exact distances. The Chinese scorn this way of planting . . . their greatest reach of imagination is employed in contriving figures where the beauty shall be great and strike the eye but without any order or disposition of parts that shall be commonly or easily observed.' After further description he concludes 'But I should hardly advise any of these attempts in the figure of gardens among us; they are adventures of too hard achievement for any common hands'.

It could be that others who read his book or had heard of the Chinese method of garden making felt more encouraged to experiment. Certainly one of the courtiers of the court of Charles II and James II, Colonel James Grahame, began, sometime in the 1690s, to plan a park beside the River Kent which flowed through his land around Levens Hall, Westmorland (now Cumbria,) and appears to have attempted something like what we would now call a landscape garden.

The landscape movement, as it eventually came to be known, really got into its stride in the second and third decades of the 18th century. Poets and writers began to ridicule the current fashion for artificiality and strict control and to advocate more natural forms of garden making. Alexander Pope coined what was to become the theme phrase of the movement 'to consult the genius of the place in all'. John Aislabie was soon making experiments at Studley Royal and Lord Carlisle, at Castle Howard in Yorkshire, was altering the schemes of his professional advisers and extending his garden to take in almost all the land that could be viewed from the magnificent new palace which Vanburgh was building for him. On the outskirts of London Lord Burlington was employing William Kent, an indifferent artist with a genius for garden design, to fashion a setting for his new Palladian villa, Chiswick House, and Kent was also soon at work for General Dormer at Rousham, Oxfordshire, as well for Lord Cobham at Stowe, Buckinghamshire, making gardens for them in the new manner, part pictorial, part poetic.

All the early landscape gardens were classical in inspiration. One can argue endlessly and probably unprofitably as to whether those who created them were inspired primarily by the pictures of landscapes they had seen when they went on the Grand Tour to Italy or by the passages they had learned from the Roman and Greek writers who loomed so large in their education. Did they really intend to create living pictures which, unlike paintings on canvas, could be viewed from many points and present a different image from each, or was their purpose to create vast stage sets in which they could imagine themselves Roman senators communing with the great warriors, and poets of classical times. Probably there was usually some element of each aided by a natural inclination towards innovation and a desire to outdo their neighbours in grandeur and modernity. Landscape gardening became the rage, at any rate in England, and many of the finest most exciting gardens were destroyed so that landscaped parks could sweep right up to the walls of mansions from which the cattle which grazed the grass were excluded by the new device of sunken fences known as ha-has.

Opposite: The Moon Ponds and Temple of Piety at Studley Royal

Since every generation regards its predecessor as old fashioned it was natural that the new landscape style evolved as the century advanced. The smooth, flowing lines and classical buildings of the early landscapes gradually gave way to rougher textures and more romantic shapes. Mock gothic ruins, rustic cottages and hermitages became fashionable and picturesqueness became the aim. The more a garden could inspire a painter to set down his easel and record its beauties the better it had achieved its purpose. The effects of light and shade were studied with increasing care and also the influence which texture could have on both, as well as on colour. The picture garden was in and, at least for a time, the patterned garden was out.

Many think that this was the greatest British gift to gardening and one of the few entirely British inventions in the world of art. It may well be so but it is also possible that more recent developments in British gardening are at least equally meritworthy. Whatever the answer to that it is undeniable that, when foreigners speak of 'the English garden' it is seldom Castle Howard, Stowe or even Stourhead which they have in mind but more likely some flowery paradise which owes more to William Robinson and Gertrude Jekyll than to Kent, Brown or Repton.

Studley Royal and Fountain's Abbey

Fountain's Abbey: the English landscape triumphant

It is remarkable how often the earliest work in a new art form proves to be the best. It is as if the very novelty of the method stimulates the executant to even greater effort and undoubtedly his imagination is not yet curbed by rules and conventions which have still to be made and sanctified by the passage of time. I have already observed that Montacute House remains one of the most beautiful houses ever built in Britain and Le Nôtre never designed any garden more completely satisfying than Vaux-le-Vicomte.

A romantic view of Fountain's Abbey taken from an old print

It is true also of Studley Royal, that grand essay in the new landscape manner made in a remote Yorkshire valley by the discredited politician John Aislabie, who was clearly a man of great daring and originality. As Chancellor of the Exchequer to George I he had helped to set in motion those financial speculations which came to be known as the South Sea Bubble and ended in complete disaster and personal disgrace. Until then Aislabie had lived mainly at Hall Barn, Buckinghamshire, much more convenient for his work in London but when the South Sea Bubble eventually burst he retired to his Yorkshire property and spent the last twenty years of his life making the garden which was to prove his most lasting title to fame.

The fact that John Aislabie never fully succumbed to the new craze for naturalness in garden making actually adds to the magic of Studley Royal. When his son, William, completed the design and took the garden right up to Fountains Abbey, a magnificent but ruined Cistercian monastery, he landscaped in the manner of Kent and Brown eschewing all formality and making the little River Skell, which is the centre and life blood of the whole scheme, meander through a meadow and burble over numerous cascades, in the most natural manner imaginable.

There was little of this rusticity in the designs for water made by his father John. He confined the river to a very long straight-sided canal with a dog leg at its upper end and used water from it to form a group of large pools on the levelled floor of the valley which contains the whole garden. The central pool is circular and is flanked by two more that are crescent shaped with a fourth that is semi-circular on the far side of the canal which itself flows so slowly down the middle that it appears to be completely still. One simple white temple with a classical pediment supported on columns is set low on the valley side to face the circular pool and another smaller domed temple is set high at the upper end of this section of the valley to command a view of the design from above.

In the telling this may sound very much like any large scale formal water garden of the 17th century except for the emphasis on classical buildings. Yet the effect of Studley Royal is totally different and is due to its situation and its surroundings. This is not a garden for the display of great wealth, still less to demonstrate man's mastery over nature or to provide a stage on which kings and courtiers can strut. Studley Royal is the first garden planned primarily for private delight and solitary meditation. It is completely concealed within a deep, heavily wooded valley a considerable distance from the mansion and completely out of sight of it.

Like Stourhead, which was not made until a quarter of a century later, Studley Royal is a garden to be visited, enjoyed for a few hours and then left to its own peace. It requires no gaily dressed crowds to complete it as the palace gardens of Le Nôtre did, and is best seen in solitude. John Aislabie's greatest triumph was to capture completely that elusive 'genius of the place' which Pope had extolled. Everything is just right and even later additions like the little gothic tower perched on the valley top above the cascade into the final lake and the handsome banqueting house (or was it intended as an orangery?) on the opposite side of the valley, slip effortlessly into place.

25

Right: The magic atmosphere of Studley Royal

Opposite: Stourhead: the Pantheon framed by the turf bridge

The water from the canal falls impressively over a high dam into a lake just outside the valley and the garden is best approached from this end if the visitor wishes to savour both its full charm and follow its historical development. This is the way that the Aislabies would have come to it from their home, Studley Royal, a mile distant on this eastern side. One can imagine them entering by the unpretentious gateway on the north side of the valley and moving quietly towards the still pools and the temple which John had dedicated to Piety. Trees and building are reflected in the water, which would have been only faintly ruffled by a single fountain (missing today) and there would be no other sound but the song of birds and the rustle of wind in the leaves.

Apparently it had always been John Aislabie's dream to carry his garden a further half mile or so up the valley to incorporate the ruins of Fountains Abbey. He was unable to effect the necessary purchase in his lifetime but after his death his son succeeded. Some think that he then worked from designs already prepared by his father. It may be so but in the absence of positive evidence to the contrary I think that they were his own ideas for they are quite different in style from those of his father. After all, by this time, the 1760's, he had all the work of Kent and much of that of Brown both to guide and constrain him. What is quite clear is that, by now, all formality has become taboo and everything must be made to appear as if it had happened without interference by the hand of man.

This upper part of the valley is concealed from the lower part by trees and high ground. It is approached by a very large curving pool, again full of reflections and delight, and the final scene is very cleverly concealed until the last moment when, rounding the bend, the abbey comes into sight and an entirely new style of landscaping is revealed. It is completely praiseworthy in its simplicity, appearing to be no more than an exceptionally beautiful brook cascading quietly through a meadow with the ruins at the far end. Inevitably at this moment the centre of interest switches from the garden to the building. I believe that is primarily what its creator intended.

Stourhead

From the moment the landscape revolution occurred many Englishmen have felt completely competent to design their own gardens. Indeed, as we have seen the revolution itself was largely made by amateurs; by John Aislabie sensing the 'genius' of his own valley in Yorkshire and of Lord Carlisle at Castle Howard, in the same county and almost at the same time, scrapping the designs of his professional advisers, John Vanburgh and the nurserymen London and Wise, and launching out on entirely novel schemes of his own with the professionals diminished to the subordinate role of providers of buildings and the architectural objects to furnish his vast landscape.

A generation later yet another amateur, Henry Hoare, grandson of Richard Hoare a wealthy 17th-century goldsmith and banker, was to create the most perfect landscape in the classical manner ever to be made anywhere in the world. To say that he consulted the genius of the place would be a gross understatement of what actually happened. For the valley with which Hoare began to work sometime in the 1730's must have seemed almost without 'genius' of any kind. Maybe had Lancelot Brown been in practice at that time he would have galloped up, looked it over and announced that it had great capability but Brown was still an under gardener at Stowe and the master plan for Stourhead, which was to convert it from a bare valley into a richly wooded Arcady, was Hoare's, with the advice of Henry Flitcroft, an architect with experience of the new Palladian style.

What he did was relatively simple; one of those strokes of genius which looks so obvious when they are completed that everyone thinks they could have done the same if only they had thought of it. The River Stour rises near to Stourhead (hence its name) and flows as a brook through the valley. Henry Hoare dammed it at several points, the major dam being where the stream circles round the valley changing its south easterly course to a south westerly one. Small dams higher up only created relatively small pools but this much larger and deeper one filled a major part of the valley with a great lake roughly triangular in shape with its face running from east to west and its apex to the north. At its south-eastern corner was the hamlet and church of Stourton and Hoare placed between it and the lake a tall and slender cross which had been made for Bristol but had been disliked by the citizens of that city as a superstitious relic. It was dismantled and lay in pieces in the crypt of Bristol Cathedral until the Dean had the bright idea that it might be just the thing for Henry Hoare's by now celebrated landscape at Stourhead.

Facing the village across the lake Fletcroft had built a large domed temple, the Pantheon, and other smaller temples were placed on the valley side overlooking the lake. Near the Pantheon was a rustic cottage

The river god

The nymph of the grot

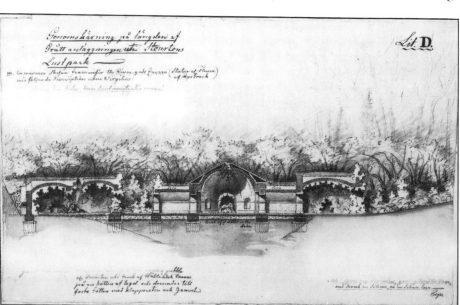

A cross section through the grotto at Stourhead drawn in 1779

28

The Hermitage in an outlying part of the garden at Stourhead

and a short distance from this a large grotto had been built right at the edge of the lake. Through a jagged, cave-like opening one can look across the lake to yet another temple and to the distant village.

Near the village the lake narrows and curls away, giving the illusion that another stream is flowing into it. Hoare seized on this as an opportunity to construct a stone bridge with five arches which, he said would make it 'look as if the river came through the village and this was the village bridge for public use'. In fact, like the rather similar bridge at Castle Howard, it lead from nowhere to nowhere and is there solely for ornament. Hoare acknowledges this saying that 'the view of the bridge, village and church altogether will be a charming Gaspard picture at that end of the water'. He was, of course, referring to Gaspard Poussin the 17th-century French artist who worked in Rome and, with Claude Lorraine and Salvator Rosa appears to have provided much of the visual inspiration for the early landscape gardeners. Hoare also states that he modelled his bridge on one designed by Palladio at Vicenza.

Here one really has the whole story of the classical English landscape. Its mainsprings were in ancient Rome and the countryside around it but a Rome already in ruins and seen largely through the eyes of painters and architects. The Italian Renaissance still dominated cultivated taste but it was now the Renaissance seen in a very different way from that of the professional 17th-century garden designers in Britain. The mansion at Stourhead, built for Henry Hoare's father (also Henry) by Colin Campbell a leading exponent of the Palladian style in architecture, was always completely out of sight of the valley in which the garden was made.

Clearly this garden, like John Aislabie's far away in Yorkshire, was meant to be visited and then left, an Arcadian paradise that would never lose by over familiarity its power to charm, but would be re-explored time and time again with renewed enchantment. Today most visitors approach Stourhead from Stourton and it is undeniable that the most spectacular view of the landscape, with the Bristol Cross and bridge in the foreground and the Pantheon in the distance reflected in the lake, is obtained from this point. Yet really to savour what Henry Hoare had planned for himself one needs to enter the garden by a totally different route, from the house above, coming across a large lawn, entering a path through woodland and then, turning a corner, suddenly seeing the Temple of Apollo apparently floating in the trees across the narrow eastern neck of the lake. Thereafter the views unfold one after another as Hoare intended and the climax occurs at the end of the tour, when the church is finally reached, and not at the beginning as it does by the usual tourist route.

I was photographing one day at Stourhead when a stranger, also carrying a camera, stopped and spoke to me. 'This is a terribly expensive garden for photographers', he said, 'I come here frequently at all seasons of the year and I always use up a lot of film'. I can think of no better recommendation for a picture garden.

Stourhead in the autumn

Alton Towers: the Chinese pagoda

Alton Towers and Scotney Castle

By the 19th century the landscape movement was beginning to run to seed. By now romanticism had taken over completely from classicism and flights of fancy tended to be increasingly uncontrolled. Alton Towers is the most startling example of what could happen under these conditions. Commenced by the 15th Earl of Shrewsbury in 1814, it was completed some 20 years later by his son, the 16th earl. By that time it is said that a million pounds had been spent on the place and the gardens contained the strangest assemblage of buildings and follies. Loudon, the great encyclo- paedist, was not amused and described it as 'in excessively bad taste . . . the mark of a morbid imagination joined to the command of unlimited resources'. It filled a valley, previously bare, in the north east corner of Staffordshire and engravings made shortly after its completion certainly show a very odd place. There was an over elaborate conservatory with seven domes, a reproduction of a monument built in 334 BC in Athens to commemorate Lysicrates, what is oddly described as an imitation of Stonehenge but is in fact a large and rather ungainly rough stone archway, a Blind Harper's cottage, a Roman Colonnade, a Grecian Temple, a Gothic (or is it Chinese?) temple or tower largely constructed of cast iron and placed on a crag where it commands the finest view of the whole garden, a fountain shaped rather like a ship's capstan and a lovely Chinese pagoda. There were streams, grottoes, topiary specimens galore, a canal and many other decorations and conceits.

31

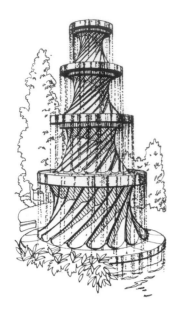

Alton Towers: the screw fountain

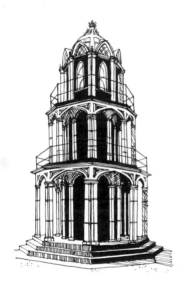

Alton Towers: the Chinese temple

To cap it all Pugin was engaged to enlarge an existing house and convert it into a fantastic Gothic mansion, all towers, pinnacles and castillations which seem totally unrelated one to another and together produce the effect of the castle of a witch or ogre. Loudon published an engraving of the place in 1833 in his book 'Cottage, Farm and Villa Architecture' (goodness knows what it was meant to contribute to that theme) and it shows most of these garden ornaments but not the mansion which was yet to be built. It also shows hundreds of trees, still too small to make much impact and as yet totally incapable of concealing the strange assemblage of follies. But, in the manner of trees, they were to go on growing and growing until now, a century and a half later, they have enveloped the whole valley in a billowy ocean of foliage in all shades of green, grey-blue, copper and purple. From this lovely forest the towers and colonnades merely peep shyly at the visitor and must be sought out, like the Chinese pagoda which, from a distance, appears simply as a small cone (it is the summit of the 65 foot high building) spurting a white jet of water into the air like a fire engine at practice. One must penetrate to the far end of the garden to see it fully and then it is revealed in all its beauty, surely the loveliest pagoda ever created outside China, standing aloof and entrancing on a little island in the centre of a pool, shrouded at times in the falling spray of the water jet which it hurls high into the sky. This is pure magic, a bewitching turquoise and white masterpiece perfect in shape and setting.

It is fascinating but idle to speculate whether either the 15th or 16th earl had sufficient vision to know that this would be the outcome of all their extravagance. Time alters gardens so greatly that it must always be in doubt just how accurately their makers can imagine what will be the outcome. But at least in another romantic garden, started a year or so after Alton Towers was completed, we do know that its creator planned with the greatest care a living picture to be enjoyed from the library and principal bedroom of his new house. This is Scotney Castle, at Lamberhurst in Kent, and since it is now the property of the National Trust, it is easy for anyone to see it. It is an enchanting garden which requires no understanding of either art or botany for its appreciation, but some knowledge of the way in which it was created certainly adds considerably to the interest of a visit.

People have been living at Scotney for at least 800 years. A castle was built there about 1380 and one of its round towers still survives intact to-day, as well as remnants of other parts of the building. The castle stood in a valley surrounded by a moat and lake fed by a brook, the Sweetbourne, discharging into the little River Bewl, which was diverted to make this possible.

Two hundred and fifty years later, when Charles I was king, much of the old castle was reconstructed as a manor house in the elegant style of that period and there successive families continued to live until the 19th century. In 1836 Scotney Castle was owned by Edward Hussey, a young gentleman then 29 years old, who was well educated and an amateur artist. For some time he had been thinking of building himself a new house on top of the hill overlooking the valley, using the old buildings as romantic objects in a picturesque landscape.

Work actually started in 1837, the very year Queen Victoria came to the throne, so it is correct to think of the new Scotney and its romantic garden as Victorian, though both are very different from the styles one usually associates with that period.

To obtain stone for his new house Mr Hussey opened a quarry just below the hilltop. When work was completed, in 1843, the lip of this quarry made a splendid vantage point from which to view the scene below. Here he made a balustraded terrace or belvedere: the quarry itself he converted into a massive rock garden planted with shrubs and herbaceous plants, for alpines had not yet come into fashion.

But it was his treatment of the old house and castle that really transformed Scotney into the gorgeous picture garden it is today. The castle was already partly ruined and needed no further attention, but the house was partially demolished with the utmost care to make it picturesque. Here were follies on a grand scale, ready made and genuine. It only remained to frame them in trees and shrubs to complete the picture Mr Hussey had already formed in his imagination.

Successive generations of the same family have continued to live at Scotney and to maintain and develop its garden, though always with the greatest care not to upset the careful balance of Edward Hussey's first composition or introduce into it glaring colours which would obtrude on its quiet good taste. Thus, though some modern hybrids have been planted in recent years, by far the greatest number of rhododendrons at Scotney Castle are of the wild species *R. ponticum* with its range of soft colours from lavender-mauve to purple. When new roses are planted they are likely to have an old-fashioned look and to be in colours sympathetic to the misty English landscapes, such as creamy-yellow 'Frühlingsgold' and madder-red 'Rosemary Rose'. However it is the choice and placing of the trees that really make Scotney Castle such an outstandingly successful landscape

The picturesque ruins of Scotney Castle

composition. A great cedar of Lebanon spreads its horizontal branches on the far valley slope as a fitting backdrop to the ruins. Attention is focused on these by columnar evergreen trees planted close to them yet not in any way concealing them. Other trees and shrubs channel the view from the belvedere and the windows of the new house, which themselves make the focal points in a second, reverse picture when they are viewed from the ruins below. Mr Christopher Hussey, the last owner of Scotney Castle, who left it to the National Trust on his death in 1970, was a leading expert on the great houses and landscapes of Britain and contributed innumerable articles on them to Country Life. In an early book 'The Picturesque', he thus described the effect the garden made on him when he was still a young man, and how it determined him to write that book. 'It happened in the library of a country house (it was Scotney Castle) built by my grandfather. Through the windows of that room you see, in a valley below, a castle partly ruined, on an island in a lake. A balustrade cresting a cliff forms the foreground, a group of Scots firs and limes, the side screens. Beyond a meadow melts in the woods, rising to a high sky line . . . On this particular evening I was pondering on the happy chance . . . of my grandfather's desertion of the old castle, his building of the new house on this particular spot and his digging of the stone for building it between the two . . . It did not occur to me that he was guided by anything more than chance and good natural taste. At that point, however, my eye ranging the mellow shelves beside me, fell on the book . . . "Sir Uvedale Price on the Picturesque". What was "the picturesque?" And what could be found to say on it filling so fat a volume?' Those questions launched Christopher Hussey on a voyage of mental exploration which was to affect his whole life. Any visitor may discover new insights into garden making by studying what Edward Hussey did at Scotney Castle and every lesson is certain to be a delight.

Opposite: Scotney Castle in the spring. A spectacular display of maples and azaleas cover the hillside

Right: A mid-18th-century watercolour of Scotney Castle before the building was ruined

Portmeirion

The romantic element in garden making has continued to attract designers right up to our own times. One of the most remarkable 20th-century examples was created by Sir Clough Williams-Ellis a famous Welsh architect who died in 1977. But Portmeirion is more than a garden; it is a dream village created in an idyllic cove on the northern shore of Traeth Bach, the almost completely land-locked estuary in North Wales where the Vale of Festiniogg comes down to the sea. Even the way in which it was created reads like a story book. About 1925 Clough William-Ellis – he was knighted in 1972 for his many services to the country – who lived in that part of Wales, was looking for a safe anchorage for his yacht. He found at Portmeirion precisely what he wanted, but to possess it he had also to purchase a derelict mid-Victorian mansion and all its equally neglected grounds. He had already written about the advantages of converting large properties for more general use and making a profit out of what might otherwise be a liability, so at Portmeirion he decided to put his theories into practice.

Since then such schemes have become commonplace, many old properties having either been converted into residential communities or been acquired by industrial companies seeking room for expansion, but Portmeirion was a pioneer in these matters and William-Ellis used methods which after a lapse of 50 years have remained unique.

What he set out to do was to exploit unashamedly the romantic qualities of the site, which is beautiful almost beyond words. This little cove is sheltered to the north by the mountains of Snowdonia. At its feet is the estuary, constantly changing in colour and pattern as the tide ebbs and flows – now leaving little but gold and silver sand, now filled with water and reflecting blue, green or grey in response to the ever-changing sky – and on the far side the hills of Harlech make a perfect backdrop. Portmeirion seems to be completely cut off from the rest of the world, screened from the sea and the bustling town of Portmadoc by the high bluff of Penrhyn Point and accessible from the land only by one tree-enclosed lane. It is the kind of smugglers' lair that abounds in Cornwall and there are echoes of Looe and Clovelly in the village that Clough Williams-Ellis created, though he drew his inspiration from many places and periods.

It is customary to speak of Portmeirion as an Italian village in Wales and compare it with Amalfi, Sorrento or other popular tourist centres, but close inspection will show that this is largely an illusion due mainly to the slender campanile which dominates the village and the free use of Mediterranean-style colour washes on the plastered walls.

In fact the buildings at Portmeirion are so diverse that they could be used for a lecture on architectural styles. Some are Baroque and Gothic, some highly sophisticated structures and others rustic almost in 'ye olde tea shoppe' manner. One which occupies a dominant position on the hillside overlooking the central recreation area looks like a classical Georgian mansion, and a formal pool in front of it is flanked by columns bearing golden statues of Hindu gods.

Portmeirion

What is remarkable is that such a heterogenous assemblage of styles can hang together so well. Well, at least part of the explanation lies in the gardens which weave in and out around the buildings and fill the whole central area. Plants, many of them exotic, are used lavishly, so that buildings and ornaments are embedded in flowers and foliage just as they are at Alton Towers. In summer the whole place seems embowered in hydrangeas, and in spring there are rhododendrons, azaleas, embothriums, lilacs and many more flowering shrubs. The effect is to provide both a setting and a screen, so that it is impossible to see all the village from any one place and yet from whatever point one looks there are trees, shrubs, terraces and lawns to link the buildings and create a delightful whole.

There is perhaps another explanation for the convincing way in which the whole village fits together. It is said that there never was an overall plan for Portmeirion, but that each house or ornament was added as requirement suggested. Now that is precisely the way in which most towns and villages develop, and though at Portmeirion the natural growth of centuries has been compressed into a few years and it was more or less completed by 1930, the development was directed by an imaginative architect with great historical knowledge and a keen eye for the picturesque. And this is really the essence of Portmeirion's success – it exploits to the full the theories of landscapers who believe that the ground itself should dictate the plan which should be used to develop the pictorial qualities of a site. Anyone who has carried a camera or a sketch pad around Portmeirion will know just how true this is, it being almost impossible to move more than a few paces without encountering a fresh and enchanting viewpoint which merits recording.

For the gardener there is also another purely horticultural delight at Portmeirion, the Gwyllt Gardens which start at the top of the valley behind the village and continue right around Penrhyn Point, with, so it is said, over 18 miles of paths, many rare trees and shrubs and wonderful views of the estuary, sea and countryside. Unhappily this area of Portmeirion has been badly neglected and few visitors ever succeed in finding their way into it. Yet it remains to be rediscovered and reclaimed and when that has been done Portmeirion will be an even better dream garden.

Opposite: Portmeirion

Right: The Garden of Peace and Contentment at Tully House

The Japanese Garden at Tully House

When Commodore Perry sailed into Tokyo Bay in 1854 he did more than open Japan to foreigners, with all the profound economic consequences that had for the Japanese people and those of the rest of the world. As a direct result of this initiative there was throughout Europe and North America a new awareness of all things Japanese, not least an interest in Japanese gardens until then virtually unknown. Western gardeners were fascinated by their apparent simplicity of design and material which concealed, rather than revealed, a mystical symbolism totally different from anything that had been attempted by any other garden makers except the Chinese.

Japanese gardens became the rage and everyone wanted to include what were conceived as Japanese features into the existing design. Few garden makers though had any real understanding of the principles which inspired the Japanese, most being concerned solely with adding a new element of picturesqueness to their gardens.

Even those garden owners sufficiently affluent to engage Japanese work-men and obtain materials direct from Japan usually succeeded in imposing their own ideas so overwhelmingly on the manner of the work that when completed, it bore little resemblance to any genuine Japanese garden. The story is frequently told of a Japanese dignitary who, being taken to view one of the new gardens, exclaimed in embarrassed amazement, 'We have nothing like it in Japan'.

He was not speaking of the garden made for Col William Hall-Walker, later to become Lord Wavertree, at Tully House, Kildare, but he might well have been, for though it is one of the most elaborate and most admired examples of this Japanese fashion, it exhibits many of the characteristics I have just described. Yet Lord Wavertree did hire a reputedly expert Japanese garden-maker named Tassa Eida who travelled to Ireland all the way from Japan with his wife and two sons and lived at Kildare for four years to supervise the work of 40 Irish gardeners.

How could so skilful a craftsman produce yet one more example of mock Japanese garden-making? I believe the explanation is to be found in an inscription for the garden which states that it 'was devised by Lord Wavertree and made by Eida and his son Meiroru between 1906 and 1910'. From this I conclude that it was Lord Wavertree who determined the broad outline of design leaving his Japanese expert to construct it and give it a convincing Japanese flavour. Unlikely as it seems, the result is one of the most successful gardens of its kind which still, 70 years later, so retains its power to beguile visitors that it is unquestioningly accepted as a genuine example of Japanese art. In every way it is an unusual garden for it sets out to tell the story of a man's life from birth to death in considerable detail.

The site is long and rather narrow, though it widens at the end farthest from the entrance. The land here is naturally moist to the point of being somewhat boggy, and there is plenty of water to feed streams and pools which, to British eyes, were an essential feature of Japanese gardens.

Visitors enter the garden by the Gate of Oblivion, presumably representing the soul seeking a body to inhabit. Almost immediately there is a rocky cave symbolising birth and then a path leading to a dark tunnel signifying the ignorance and incomprehension of the infant. But the tunnel passes beneath the Hill of Learning to which the growing child has access if he chooses.

Soon he must return to level ground to pursue his way beside a winding stream until he reaches a three-way parting of roads. To the left the straight path of austere living leads to batchelordom and to the right a flowery way covered in spring with cherry blossom invites him to a life of self-indulgence. He chooses the middle path which quickly leads him to the Island of Joy and Wonder, with marriage as his reward and a broken stone bridge across the stream to indicate that he has made a new start in life. For a while all is harmony but soon difficulties appear. There are differences of opinion between him and his wife and a steep Hill of Ambition to be climbed. Arriving at the top he spies a Well of Wisdom which he seeks to reach but the road is barred by the stream, this time with no bridge, not even a broken one, to allow him to cross. He must retrace his steps and try other paths, but by the time he does at last attain his goal life is drawing to a close. He and his wife enter a Garden of Peace and Contentment with a level lawn, shady trees and a wide, slow moving stream. The Gateway of Eternity brings their joint pilgrimage to its close.

There can be few gardens which set out to tell a story of any kind, let alone such an elaborate one as this. I must confess that, without constant reference to the guidebook, I found it impossible to determine what I was

The Geisha house

supposed to learn from my surroundings. I soon gave up and spent the rest of my time just enjoying the very attractive garden.

All the expected Japanese features are there, including a red lacquered half-moon bridge and a well-constructed Geisha house, which was sent from Japan together with the numerous stone ornaments which decorate the garden. There are some remarkable examples of bonsai also originating from Japan, several reputed to be very old. Rock work is used boldly to create the impression of high mountains, and water is handled with great charm. The final Garden of Peace and Contentment is backed by beautiful cherry trees and most of the planting has a genuine Japanese flavour though by no means all are native Japanese species.

Lord Wavertree's other major interest was horse-breeding and he established a stud farm at Tully House which by 1915 had become the British National Stud. In 1966 it was handed over to the Irish Government and is now the Irish National Stud. The house in which Tassa Eide once lived has become a Racing Apprentice Centre. But fortunately none of this has interfered with the maintenance of the garden which is impeccably preserved and is open daily from Easter to the end of October. It is one of the best examples in the British Isles of a fashion in garden-making which for a time must have appeared very important, but which was too rigid and disciplined to make any great impact on the mainstream of British garden design and our insatiable yearning for experiment and variety.

Tully House: the half-moon bridge

Planters
by the
Sea

*I*t is natural for writers to tidy history up; to attempt to divide the ages into neat compartments giving each a name, a beginning and an end as though things really worked like that. Of course they do not, least of all in the world of arts and crafts to which garden making belongs. Though I have written about 17th-century gardens as if this were a period entirely devoted to formality and the 18th century as if all its gardens were landscapes, in each period there were many garden makers who refused to conform. Neither type of garden, formally patterned or artistically conceived, offered great scope for variety in planting and yet from mediaeval times there were always some gardeners who were more interested in plants than in designs.

As the years passed and travellers ventured even further afield, what had begun as a trickle of new plants from foreign places gradually grew into a flood. By the close of the 18th century the number of species available to plant lovers was already numbered in thousands and new ones were arriving all the time.

This enormous influx of unfamiliar plants not only fascinated gardeners to such a degree that many devoted their whole time to collecting as many as possible and mastering their cultivation, but also stimulated some to attempt to produce entirely new types previously unknown in the wild. Plant breeding became fashionable and was practised by many amateurs interested only in the results they might achieve, as well as by professionals concerned with profit as well as with novelty.

Plants became the rage and since the fashionable garden styles did not make much provision for them, the landscapes being largely stocked with the cheapest and most readily available trees and shrubs that would produce the required visual effects and the formal gardens with those that could be suitably trained or restricted, new styles of garden making were invented to suit the new needs. Since the guiding principle in these was to make plants happy, the term 'gardenesque' has been used for some aspects of this development but it is an awkward term not generally understood by present day gardeners and really only applicable to one of many styles which became fashionable in the 19th century. As this was a period of

Opposite: View from Dereen to Kilmackillogue Harbour

Right: Rhododendron *'Lady Roseberry'*

*View from Inverewe across
Loch Ewe*

experiment in which many ideas were tried out, I prefer to lump all those planners who had plants mainly in mind as 'the planters'. Those who were interested mainly in trees planted arboretums and pinetums; those who were fascinated by the more tender plants coming from South Africa, India, Central and South America, tropical Asia and Australasia either sought to perfect conservatories and other glasshouses as well as the means of heating them, or looked for specially favourable climates in which to grow them outdoors; and those mainly interested in hybrids were quite content to grow their plants in beds of any size and shape that made cultivation easy.

It is facile to speak of 'Victorian gardens' and think that one has a clear idea of what they were like. It is much more difficult to grasp the multiplicity of aims and styles that actually existed side by side in this exuberant, self-confident period. Nor is it even sensible to separate gardens made in Victoria's reign from those that came before and after as if the great queen herself influenced their design and content. Change was already in process long before Victoria came to the throne. More than half a century earlier Princess Augusta was beginning to make a private botanical collection at Kew House, which Queen Victoria was to give to the nation as the basis of the Royal Botanic Garden, Kew. On a sunny hillside at Killerton, near Exeter, Sir Thomas Acland was beginning, in the 1790's, to plant exotic trees in

44

considerable numbers and his professional assistant was a Scottish gardener, John Veitch, who later founded a nursery destined to grow into the most famous and prestigious in Britain and the source of much of the material which the planters were so eager to grow.

By the 1820's Charles Fowler was building at Syon for the Duke of Northumberland a great curving conservatory which provided far better conditions for tender plants than the orangeries which it superseded, but even this lovely building was soon eclipsed as a means of providing controllable climatic conditions by the superlative buildings of Joseph Paxton at Chatsworth and Decimus Burton at Kew. In the former the royal water lily flowered for the first time in Britain and in the Kew Palm House exotic palms and cycads grew to their full size as if in their native tropics.

As the century advanced new races of roses appeared including the controversial hybrid teas which were, for better or worse, destined to give roses an entirely new role as bedding plants. Dahlias, gladioli and begonias developed as wholly artificial species, as domesticated and dependent on man for survival as the cattle and the corn in the fields.

Herbaceous borders were invented as a means of displaying the multitudinous herbaceous perennials that were becoming available mostly from the Northern Hemisphere. Rock gardens, originally conceived as picturesque features in romantic settings changed their purpose and style and became homes, for a while, for the alpine plants newly discovered by Victorian gentry who had opened up Switzerland as a playground for the rich.

By the 1850's rhododendrons and azaleas were beginning to take gardeners by storm, and before the century was out so many people were breeding so many new varieties that their gardens could no longer contain them. The plants burst out into the surrounding coppices and woodlands which they soon filled with their exotic flowers to the wonderment of the public at large and the annoyance of purists, who complained that the British countryside was being desecrated by these exotic intruders.

Orchid growers went off on paths of their own so specialised that they often absorbed their whole attention to the exclusion of any other plants. Some were prepared to pay immense sums for exclusive new varieties and a few were by no means pleased when improved methods of propagation greatly increased the rate of increase and reduced the price so much that almost anyone could afford to grow good orchids.

The zest for new plants has continued right up to the present day, though it has ceased to be the most characteristic feature of our gardens as it undoubtedly was of most gardens during most of the 19th century. The Victorians were the great innovators, bursting with enthusiasm and with the whole world open to them. We live in more difficult times; many of our horticulturally most exciting countries separated by wars and national prejudices; our home efforts hamstrung by the fears of conservationists; lacking any clear sense of direction but with the advantage of three centuries of highly diversified garden making to guide us.

Let us take a closer look at some of the outstanding 19th-century achievements and begin with one very special development of that period. For it was then that gardeners began to discover what are now known as micro-climates, those pockets or belts of land in which, for some local reason, climatic conditions differ markedly from the norm. They may be warmer or colder, moister or drier, with greater or less light intensity and with soils showing very different physical properties. All could be of use to the new race of plant lovers seeking suitable conditions for new species from foreign countries but none proved more fruitful of remarkable collections than the maritime gardens, particularly those of the westerly coasts of the British Isles. Gardeners discovered that in some of these places, if suitable protection could be provided from the salt-laden gales which swept across them and adequate improvement could be made to the usually poor soil with which nature had endowed them, they had, ready made, and without further expense, climatic conditions comparable with those that had previously been created in orangeries and conservatories. The great age of the seaside garden had commenced.

The Neptune steps in Tresco Abbey gardens

The arch in Tresco Abbey gardens; the only remnant of the old Cistercian Priory

Tresco Abbey

On the tiny island of Tresco in the Isles of Scilly is a garden so fabulous that, once within its protective tree belt, it is easy to imagine one has been magically transported to the Pacific. Even the little group of islands ranged more or less in a circle around shallow water amid the Atlantic deep, contributes to the illusion that these are islands encircling a tropical lagoon.

The story of the creation of this fantastic garden is one of the great romances of English horticulture. It was due, in the first place, to the vision of one remarkable man, Augustus Smith, but his dream could not have been fully realised without the continuing labours of four generations of his descendants who even to the present day, despite all the difficulties imposed by taxation and inflation, continue to maintain and improve the garden without seeking public assistance.

Augustus Smith could be described as an autocratic Victorian do-gooder though, in fact, he was in full possession of all the islands several years before Victoria came to the throne. He introduced universal education by the simple expedient of charging 1d a day for attending school and 3d for staying away. At that time the islands were barren and poverty stricken, the inhabitants scraping a living mainly by fishing, smuggling and wrecking. Today the islands are prosperous and beautiful, a Mecca for tourists for whom Tresco Abbey garden is one of the essential wonders to be enjoyed during their stay.

47

Augustus Smith chose Tresco for his personal home because he wanted the maximum of privacy. It is one of the smaller islands, little more than two miles long and barely a mile wide and at the time of his purchase in 1834 it must have been a singularly unattractive place. No trees grew on it nor even gorse bushes, which Smith was quick to introduce. There was no building of any size, although there had once been a monastery of which a solitary arch within the garden remains as a reminder. The monks chose this spot because there is abundant fresh water here and it was probably this, and the fact that it is a little sheltered from north and west by a low ridge, that made Smith select this area for his new mansion which he called Tresco Abbey; for already he had conceived the idea of making a garden in this unlikely place.

He was one of the first to appreciate the advantages which the extreme south west of Britain might have for the cultivation outdoors of many plants normally grown in glasshouses, but he also realised that if any but the most wind resistant were to be grown he must provide shelter from Atlantic gales. The island is washed by the Gulf Stream Drift, which is not exactly warm, as many people imagine, but scarcely changes temperature at all from a chilly 10 to 12°C (50 to 53°F) winter and summer. The sunshine is so clear that it can skin you in a few hours. The hazard for plants is the wind which sweeps in from the Atlantic with unbelievable fury.

So Augustus Smith built his house and planted miscellaneous trees in the hope that some would remain alive. While he waited for them to grow he filled his garden with the toughest palms and succulent plants from the Canary Islands and other places in which plants have learned to adapt themselves to similar hazards.

His shelter belt progressed slowly but it was not until shortly before his death in 1874 that he observed two trees outstripping all the others. It was a remarkable discovery, not only for Tresco but for maritime gardens throughout Britain.

For the trees were the Monterey pine and the Monterey cypress, *Pinus radiata* and *Cypressus macrocarpa*, two evergreen conifers that in the wild had become almost extinct, except in a small area on the coast of California, but in cultivation were destined to thrive and give shelter to gardens in many parts of the world. Both are unaffected by salt laden gales and grow rapidly in the most exposed places so long as they do not have to endure severe frost. It was precisely what Tresco Abbey needed, and soon the woodland round the garden was replanted almost entirely with these two trees. As they grew upwards the flora within the garden could be made increasingly varied and tropical.

Today it can rival many subtropical botanic gardens and plants are constantly being sent from such places as Kew to test their potentiality for survival in such very special, man-made mini-climates as this. Though plants from all parts of the world can be found at Tresco, the garden is particularly rich in plants from the southern hemisphere. The moderate rainfall and high light intensity suit many plants from Australasia, South Africa and the drier regions of Central and South America. Plants are in flower at Tresco during every month of the year and there is no season at which it is not a fascinating place for plant lovers to visit. Nevertheless, June

Puya chiloensis *growing at Tresco Abbey*

and July are its peak months and it is then that some of the most exotic blooms can be seen. They will include stiff green and yellow spikes of *Puya chilensis* and *P. alpestris* unfolding its even more startling peacock-blue spires. Great echiums, some of them wild species from the Canary Islands, others handsome hybrids between them, created at Tresco, will be flowering all over the garden; so will aeoniums from the Canary Islands, mesembryanthemums, aloes, pelargoniums and watsonias from South Africa, strange fuchsias and bomarias from South America, 30 feet furcraeas from Central America, kennedyas from Australia and hundreds more.

Most remarkable of all are the meterosideros from New Zealand, some of them great evergreen trees which throw out aerial roots even from branches high above the ground. In their descent they may strangle other trees in their path and eventually these strange roots grow into trunks, so that, in time, one tree can resemble a grove. At their peak the scarlet flowers of the biggest species can be seen like beacons from St Mary two miles distant across that lagoon-like stretch of water. It is the island on which one must land by sea or air on one's way to Tresco.

Launches ply frequently between the islands, and Tresco itself has two excellent hotels, though they get fully booked for the high season; yet out of season it is still a wonderland. I have been there in early March and found it full of Australian acacias and South African heaths as well as strange proteas and banksias from both countries, and I have also been there in autumn to admire late-flowering bulbs of many kinds, kniphofias, fuchsias and the pelargoniums which never seem to tire of flowering.

There is no other garden quite like it anywhere in the British Isles, and quite probably not anywhere else in the world because of its unique climate and the dedicated plant collecting of its owners for well over a hundred years.

Inverewe

Nearly 30 years after Augustus Smith purchased the Isles of Scilly, in 1862 to be exact, a Scot was making a similar decision about a tiny peninsula on the north-west coast of Scotland. Inverewe and Tresco have three things in common; both are exposed to the full fury of Atlantic gales, both are washed by water kept at a very equable temperature by the Gulf Stream Drift and neither had much vegetation until their new owners took them in hand. In other respects they are very different. In Inverewe, Poolewe there is none of the overpowering sunlight that characterises the clear air of the Isles of Scilly and the day length varies much more between winter and summer. Loch Ewe, into which the little peninsula juts, is a region of cloud, rain and mists as well as of wind. Mountains back it to the south and east but they do not ameliorate the conditions since the long valley of Loch Maree funnels the south easterlies directly on to Poolewe. From every point of view it is an even more unlikely spot than Tresco in which to make a garden, still more one composed mainly of exotic plants. Yet that is precisely what Osgood MacKenzie set out to do and unlike Augustus Smith, nearly 600 miles to the south, he lived long enough to see his dream come true. By the time he died in 1922 his shelter belts were mature and his garden was full of rare rhododendrons, meconopsis, primulas and celmisias, acacias, eucalyptus and tree ferns from Australia and New Zealand grew cheek by jowl with umbrella-leaved gunneras and elegant eucryphias from South America, tree magnolias and lily of the valley shrubs (pieris) from China and hydrangeas from Japan.

At first glance there seemed to be no limit to what might be grown, but close inspection revealed a fundamental difference between the flora at Inverewe and that of Tresco. Here in the misty north it was the moisture-loving plants that were succeeding. There was an almost complete absence of the succulents which figure so prominently at Tresco and of the sun lovers and those plants that only flower when days are warm yet nights are quite long. Summer days at Inverewe are rarely very hot and whether warm or cold they seem to go on for ever with real darkness confined to a few brief hours around midnight. That kind of thing can upset plants that grow in equatorial countries.

Opposite: Inverewe gardens encircled by sea and mountains

Right: Asiatic primulas growing in an open glade at Inverewe

Far right: Meconopsis grandis

After Osgood MacKenzie's death, his daughter Mrs Marie T. Sawyer continued to tend Inverewe with loving care for a further thirty years and it was not until 1952, just a year before she died, that she decided to hand her father's creation to the National Trust for Scotland. Though it is so remote the Trust was happy to accept the gift and it has proved a wise choice for Inverewe has become a favourite place for tourists as well as for dedicated gardeners. It has continued to prosper under the Trust's care and has actually benefited from the free exchange of plants between one Trust garden and another coupled with skilful management and adequate financial backing.

Today Inverewe is one of the most beautiful as well as one of the most remarkable gardens in the British Isles. In some ways this is unusual for a place that began as a collector's garden for collectors tend to be more interested in making their treasures happy than in producing beautiful landscapes or carefully considered designs. But in a place such as Inverewe it was almost impossible to go wrong. The early shelter belts, made here mainly with Scots pine and the rather similar Corsican pine, did not merely grow around the perimeter of the garden, as at Tresco, but spread across it forming a more or less continuous woodland which established the style of the garden. The nature of the site, steep and irregular, ensured that there would be constant variety of outlook, with sometimes a peep of the loch or the mountains through the trees and often merely a path winding up or down between lovely plants, always enticing the visitor to proceed further.

Because the ground is so irregular and the paths so steep and winding, Inverewe seems to be a very much larger garden than it is. It is also a very easy garden in which to lose all sense of direction and become temporarily lost, though arrows placed at key junctions soon set the visitor off on the right track again and the sea, house and excellent restaurant are never very far away.

Only in the front of the house is there any hint of formality and this more the formality of a well-ordered modern garden, with well-trimmed lawn, well-stocked herbaceous border and a fascinating dry wall full of small plants. The dry wall, a raised rock bed, separates the lawn from the rock garden made on a steep bank which drops to the sea. It is a relatively new feature of the garden and a most valuable one, as it has made it possible to grow a lot of rare or difficult rock or alpine plants which would soon get smothered elsewhere. The rock garden itself, though mainly filled with more robust plants, is also excellent both as a collection and a very beautiful feature. A large eucalyptus tree leans across the path at what seems a dangerous angle but never seems to slip any further. It makes a handsome background to almost any photograph of the rock bank looking east.

One tends to think of plant collectors as having little interest in the more practical side of gardening such as growing fruit and vegetables. Perhaps it is that collectors tend to regard these things as of little interest to their friends and so hide them away behind walls or screens. At Inverewe there is neither opportunity nor inclination to do any such thing. The only practical site for the kitchen garden was between the entrance drive and the sea and although it is walled in the manner of all good Scottish kitchen gardens it is so well below the level of the drive that in places one looks right down onto it. In its way it is as remarkable as the garden of rare plants. The cultivation is superb, everything is in apple-pie order and the crops always seem weeks ahead of anything I can manage to grow in Sussex. And, of course, as a normal Scottish bonus, there are flowers all through the vegetable garden; long borders of them full of colour and with lots of plants to admire and not a few that may be a puzzle to name unless you have a very good knowledge of herbaceous perennials and annuals.

When the woodland garden has been fully explored and admired it is worth walking back through this kitchen garden on the way to the restaurant, information centre and spacious car park. A guide can be purchased at the information centre. It not only includes a map, a history of the garden and a step by step tour, but also a catalogue of over 850 of the plants that grow at Inverewe. Even this is not complete but it is a great help in finding special plants one wishes to see and identifying those (and they are usually numerous) that one does not know, since the names are grouped according to the particular areas of the garden in which the plants grow.

Even at Inverewe there are plants in flower throughout the year though naturally not so many of them in winter as in Tresco. The best time to visit Inverewe is from late April until early August with the peak display in May and early June. But the setting is so beautiful and the planting so unusual that I would visit this garden at any time rather than miss it altogether.

Rossdohan Island and Derreen

It was not only on, or off, the west coast of Britain that the plant lovers found ideal climatic conditions. Ireland could also offer them, especially in the deep estuaries of her own Atlantic coast. To those who do not know Ireland fairly well it will not be obvious that the Kenmare River is not a river but one of these estuaries, a particular turbulent one, on the south-west coast where Co. Kerry meets Co. Cork. At its mouth it is about five miles wide and it tapers eastwards for about 25 miles to the little town of Kenmare where the Roughty River and the Sheen River flow into it. To the north are Macgillycuddy's Reeks, to the south the Slieve Miskish and Cara Mountains.

Midway in this funnel for Atlantic gales are two of the most remarkable plant collections in the British Isles, Rossdohan Island to the north and Derreen to the south. It is possible to see one from the other, and there are some similarities between the plants that grow in them, yet there is a marked difference between the climatic conditions of the two gardens. Both have a rainfall in the 30 inch range and a complete absence of severe frost. But Rossdohan Island juts out into the estuary and is fully exposed to all westerly gales whereas Derreen is in a deep, much-indented inlet, known as Kilmackillogue Harbour, and so is relatively sheltered.

By coincidence, planting started in both these remote places in 1870. At Rossdohan Island it was Samuel Thomas Heard, a retired surgeon-major who had served in the Indian army, who set to work, and across the estuary at Derreen it was the 5th Marquess of Lansdowne. The tasks that confronted them were markedly different and reflected the contrast in climate. According to an account in Curtis's Botanical Magazine for 1915, a volume dedicated to Samuel Heard, there was only one hawthorn bush on Rossdohan Island when he purchased it, and he had to provide some shelter before contemplating making a garden. This he did first by planting escallonias, a rather unusual choice. The Monterey cypress and Monterey pine, *Cupressus macrocarpa* and *Pinus radiata*, followed quickly, but perhaps the most successful shelter plant was *Acacia melanoxylon*, some plants of which are now over 50 feet high and are said to flower well. It was an early indication that Australasian plants were eventually going to dominate this garden.

At Derreen the Marquess found so much native scrub oak and holly that he had to clear a lot to make room for exotic plants of his choice.

One of the most remarkable successes in both gardens has been with Australian tree ferns. These enjoy the moist, mild air and acid soil so much that they are completely naturalised. They are constantly renewing them-

*Looking across the Kenmare
River to Dereen from
Rossdohan Island*

*Inset left: Tree ferns
flourishing at Rossdohan*

Inset right: Dicksonia
antarctica *growing at Dereen*

selves by self-sown spores which come up all over the place, but at Derreen particularly in the drainage ditches. Here it is *Dicksonia antarctica* that has taken charge, and there are some very large specimens growing in groves so that one walks beneath them as in a sub-tropical jungle. At Rossdohan dicksonia is joined by the silver tree fern, *Cyathea dealbata*, which spreads by sporelings as freely as the dicksonia.

Because of their contrasted situation and also, perhaps, on account of their owner's individual ideas as to what a garden should be, the two collections have developed very differently. Derreen, which now belongs to the Hon. David Bigham, is the more obviously designed of the two, especially around the house where there are undulating lawns leading to wide grassed vistas between coppices of trees and shrubs. The house stands on the highest point of the 90-acre peninsula; there a huge dome-shaped outcrop of rock shields it from the estuary and makes a striking landscape feature. There are a number of fine conifers, some planted as specimens, some in small groups. One could call it a woodland-glade garden. There are a lot of rhododendrons, some of them grown to great size.

Various eucalyptus species grow well and a big *Embothrium coccineum lanceolatum* grows between the house and the sea. There is also one of the tallest specimens of *Cryptomeria japonica elegans* in the British Isles, but unhappily this now lies at an awkward angle, almost blocking one of the narrower paths which wind through the outlying parts of the garden. Here one is often hemmed in by dense hedges of gaultheria and pernettya which grow so freely that they have to be drastically cut back occasionally.

Rossdohan never seems to have had any overall plan but to have grown up more or less spontaneously, as shelter from gales could be provided.

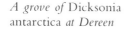
A grove of Dicksonia antarctica *at Dereen*

But in 1873 Surgeon-Major Heard did build a stone house on a raised terrace looking up the estuary, and close to this a later owner, Nicholas I. Fitzgerald, made a long sunken garden with lily pool. Heard's house was destroyed by fire in 1922 shortly after his death. For the next 15 years the island was uninhabited and cattle grazed over it. Mr Fitzgerald purchased it in 1937 and rebuilt the house a year later, to a design by Michael Scott, in the Dutch colonial style with a thatched roof. He also cleared the garden paths and generally brought good order back to the place but does not seem to have done much new planting except in the sunken garden. He sold Rossdohan in 1954 to a Mr Johnson and six months later the house was again burned down.

The present owners are Ralph (President of the Irish Horticultural Society) and Philip Walker. They bought Rossdohan Island in 1955 and have maintained and further extended this beautiful place. As a result it is probably now a finer garden than at any time in its century-long history.

One of the most impressive things about Rossdohan is the size of almost all the plants that grow in it. All previous ideas of scale have to be abandoned in this astonishing place. Here are the biggest specimens of *Clethra arborea* in the British Isles, one, according to Bean's 'Trees and Shrubs Hardy in the British Isles', 51 feet high in 1966 and two others 36 feet and 25 feet. *Olearia argyrophylla*, the muskwood of New South Wales, is well over 30 feet high and covers itself in large clusters of off-white flowers. The rough bark of its trunks make lodging places for the tender East Indian fern *Polypodium scolopendria* which covers it with green fronds. *Olearia argyrophylla* is itself regarded as tender, but here it is so much at home that its self-sown seedlings are widely distributed.

The yellow *Erica pageana* and pink *E. hirtifolia* thrive, woodwardias grow all over the place, there are fine plants of *Blechnum tabulare* and huge specimens of *Beschorneria yuccoides* with snaking, pink-bracted flower spikes up to 15 feet in length. Some eucalyptus are enormous, particularly *Eucalyptus globulus*.

One can admire quite large hakeas that are only two years old from seed; tall branching specimens of *Dracaena reflexa*; *Suttonia salicina* with with narrow glossy leaves and reddish shoots; red-flowered correas grown from Australian seed; *Fuchsia excorticata* 20 feet high; leptospermums up to 40 feet and *Mitraria coccinea*, a rare Chilean evergreen climber, 40 feet up among the trees.

There is a considerable collection of bamboos and *Restio subverticillata*, the South African rope grass which looks like a slender bamboo, grows well. A shrubby species of strobilanthes thrives and is not cut down even when there is some frost. Casuarinas, several species of podocarpus, *Brachyglottis repanda* and banksias are other plants which thrive here.

All accounts of Rossdohan Island speak of the repeated havoc caused by Atlantic gales, one of which is said to have destroyed more than a thousand trees, but each time the garden has recovered from these disasters in the most remarkable way. No sign of damage persists for long and the trees are so dense that it seems impossible there could ever have been any more. Here, even more than at Derreen, one gets the impression of walking in a jungle, and it is a very thrilling experience.

Achamore House

To start when nearly 60 to make a great collection of exotic plants is unusual. To purchase for this express purpose an island in the Atlantic must surely be unique. Yet this is precisely what Lt-Col Sir James Horlick, Bt did and the garden that he began to plant in 1944 on the island of Gigha had attained complete maturity by the time of his death in 1973.

For many years Sir James had been gaining skill as a plantsman at Titness Park, near Henley-on-Thames, Berkshire. Here he had acquired a special love of rhododendrons and had started to breed new varieties with considerable success. But excellent though conditions in that part of Berkshire are for the tougher rhododendron species and hybrids, the climate is too cold for the more tender kinds and too dry for the magnificent large-leaved species. It was to enable him to extend his collection to include practically any rhododendron that can reasonably be expected to grow anywhere in the British Isles, that Sir James began to explore the possibilities of making a new garden on the west coast of Scotland or on one of the offshore islands. Here the air is moist, the rainfall mainly high and the climate equable thanks to the amelioating influence of the Gulf Stream Drift.

First he inspected a site at Islay, then one on the mainland in northern Argyll, but it was the tiny island of Gigha with its satellite islets of Cara and Gigalum that really captivated him. Gigha lies three miles off the coast of Kintyre on the way to Islay. It is six miles long, a bare one and a half across at its widest. Shaped rather like a basking whale, its highest spot 331 feet Creag Bhan, looks a puny mound against the 2,500 feet Paps of Jura, which form the spectacular backdrop to it as one is ferried across from Tayinloan.

Achamore House, home for more than a century of successive lairds of Gigha, faces the mainland and is a little protected from the Atlantic by the central spine of the hill. Early in the century a previous owner planted many trees around the house, partly no doubt for further shelter, but also probably as cover for game. The trees have not grown particularly well, for the gales are too fierce and salt laden and the soil too acid to suit most deciduous species. All the same, sycamore, elm, ash and alder have survived, together with Scots and Corsican pine to give winter protection and around the house some big cordylines create a tropical appearance on a sunny day.

In fact there is nothing remotely tropical about the climate of Gigha with its short winter days, relatively low light intensity and summer mean temperature rather under than over 14°C (56°F). It was not, perhaps, what most people would have considered an ideal site for a garden, but it was precisely what Sir James Horlick wanted, and in 1944 he became the new laird of Gigha.

Because many rhododendrons thrive best in thin woodland it is largely a woodland garden that Sir James Horlick created around Achamore House, though by no means exclusively so. On my first visit I was surprised by the amount of open space and the pleasant landscaping, for I

Opposite: Rhododendrons in the woodland at Achamore House

was well aware that this was the garden of a great collector, and the art of making difficult plants happy does not always fit well with the sister art of garden design. Moreover I had been warned that this was not an easy garden to photograph, and even the excellent guide book seemed a little defensive on this. 'This garden,' it proclaims, 'is not one of great landscapes; it is one in which the plants invite individual inspection, and has the air of being made for plants rather than for human indulgence in them.'

Well, may be so, but having seen Gigha twice at different times of the year and talked to visitors in the garden I am convinced that it has a much wider appeal than this judgment might lead one to suppose. Of course, some knowledge of plants will add to the pleasure of a visit; but anyone who loves gardens, however ignorant of the names of plants or the places from which they come, will find delight here, and not simply when the rhododendrons and azaleas are in bloom, magnificent though they are. For in Sir James's garden there are many other plants besides rhododendrons and many lovely garden scenes.

Though the popular varieties of *Camellia japonica* do not succeed particularly well, apparently for lack of light and warmth, the new hybrids between these camellias and the Chinese species, *Camellia saluenensis* grow fast and flower freely. In one place there is a whole grove of the double-flowered pink 'Donation', which is one of the loveliest things I have ever seen in any garden, and other varieties of *C. williamsii*, as these hybrids are collectively named, grow equally well on Gigha.

Camellia williamsii
'*Donation*'

It was part of the secret of Sir James's success as a garden maker that he planted many things in bold groups. If one arrives in June one is greeted by great drifts of deciduous azaleas beside the curving drive to the house. Here are no mixed or clashing colours, but well-spaced groups of orange yellow and white with ample areas of grass between and a cool background of massed trees and shrubs, many of them rare.

Passing the house and entering the large walled garden, the June visitor will find roses already beginning to bloom in big blocks of a kind; and continuing on through a little gate to the path that follows the line of the protecting hillside he will be intoxicated by the rich perfume of large drifts of the well-named *Rhododendron fragrantissimum*. This lovely hybrid is too tender for most British gardens, but here it covers considerable banks with spicily-scented, snow-white bloom. This is one of the most sheltered parts of the gardens where visitors who come early will find such tender rarities as daffodil-yellow *Rhododendron burmanicum*, primrose *R. johnstoneanum* in both single- and double-flowered forms, white *R. lindleyi* with scented, trumpet-shaped flowers like white lilies, and a gorgeous crimson form of the tree rhododendron, *R. arboreum*.

In June, too, all the damper places are filled with candelabra primulas, white, pink and magenta, which never need to be replanted since they seed themselves everywhere and have frequently to be reduced to prevent them becoming a nuisance. This, of course, is not uncommon in west-coast gardens, in which all the Asiatic primroses thrive. Nor is it astonishing to see considerable areas covered by the huge umbrella leaves of gunnera, for this Chilean perennial delights in moist, cool, but relatively frost-free places such as Gigha provides so generously.

What is more unexpected is to find the distinctly tender and, I had supposed, warmth-loving *Cordyline indivisa*, the palm-like 'dracaena' of many a home countries conservatory, thriving in the open air, and the strange Mexican beschorneria with its yucca-like leaves and snaking pink flower spikes behaving almost as a weed.

Still later in the year there are mock oranges (philadelphus) to fill the air with perfume, to be followed by eucryphias, hebes, hydrangeas and viburnums in great variety. White and carmine leptospermums from New Zealand grow well, and so does the uncommon waratah, *Telopea speciosissima*, an Australian member of the protea family. It makes one wonder whether the South African proteas and leucodendrons could themselves be made to thrive, but Gigha is no Tresco, for all its winter mildness and probably the lack of really bright light would prove fatal. Yet a doubt lingers, for with plants theory and practice so seldom go hand in hand.

As great gardens go, Achamore is not particularly large, perhaps only a little over 50 acres, though it is difficult to be precise since it tends to grow year by year. But the impression left on visitors is of a much greater area. This is mainly because of the way in which it has been subdivided with hedges and shelter belts of senecio, escallonia, elaeagnus, griselinia and leyland cypress to provide the maximum protection from salt-laden gales and the greatest variety in micro-climates to suit fussy plants. Some expecially choice specimens actually inhabit arboreal niches of their own, while others are grouped in compounds varying in size and shape. It is almost as if a modern compartment garden on the Hidcote or Sissinghurst

Masses of daffodils at Achamore House in the spring

pattern had been created in a woodland with all formality banished and paths largely replaced by tracks. Even in the more open spaces one seldom gets a glimpse of the house or any other readily recognisable object so that it is easy to lose all sense of direction, as in a maze.

Because of the wind problem it has been necessary to keep open vistas to a minimum, but there is one splendid view eastwards from the relatively high ground outside the walled garden over the lawns that flank the drive to the sea and the high moorlands of Kintyre. There are also numerous closed vistas within the woodland, notably around the pools and the area known as the Theatre Garden and the Triangle. Here pictures on a more restricted scale have been formed with turf, water and plants within a framework of trees, and very beautiful they are. Below the house there is also a large sweep of rough mown grass that is covered in spring with daffodils flanked by a veritable thicket of the Formosan *Pieris taiwanensis* covered with flowers like neat bouquets of lily of the valley.

It has been suggested that such places as this, in which an attempt is made to bring together plants from all parts of the world should be known as paradise gardens. It seems an appropriate title for the garden that has been created on the island of Gigha.

University College of Wales

It is fortunate for garden lovers that, as private wealth decreases, public bodies of one kind and another have been increasingly willing to engage in creative garden making. Municipalities improve their parks, urban developers employ the best landscape architects and even industrialists are discovering that good planting can be a good investment by improving their image with both the public and their employees. But in recent years

Opposite: Candelabra primulas around the pond at Achamore House

Right: The garden at Plas Penglais at the University College of Wales

Planting suggested by Brenda Colvin on the university campus

some of the most interesting work of all has been done by universities and colleges. One of these is to be found at the University College of Wales, Aberystwyth.

As so often happens it is the difficulties of the task that have stimulated the imagination of the planners and spurred them to produce planting of considerable distinction. Two separate but adjacent gardens have been created, one in the campus of the university college the other, separated from it by a main road, as a botany garden. The two sites are barely a mile from the sea but some 200 feet above it. They are fully exposed to salt laden gales from the west and, in winter, to bitter winds from the east sweeping down from snow covered hills on to the unprotected surface of the coastal belt. When the original 87 acres was purchased in 1929 by Sir Joseph Davies and given to the university college as a gift, it was quite unprotected by trees and though the Penglais estate of about 25 acres, acquired in 1946 for the Botany Garden, was the park of a private mansion, Plas Penglais, it was in a derelict state and required almost complete replanting. So from the outset the planners had to think for themselves with no existing guidelines and not a great deal of help from either site or soil.

The first problem was to determine what would thrive in these exposed maritime and hill conditions on soil that is mostly clay, moisture retentive and acid, and even where it is more porous is shallow and overlies rock which impedes drainage.

So a careful study was made by the planners of some other coastal gardens, especially in the west and south, and an extensive list was prepared of plants that seemed likely to be suitable. In the succeeding years only about thirty of these have been withdrawn as not coming up to expectations but there have been more than ninety additions, many of them plants that are little known in other British gardens or might seem unsuitable for such a difficult situation. In particular a really impressive collection has been established of trees and shrubs from the Southern Hemisphere with particular emphasis on South America and Australasia.

Only two of the university college buildings are pre-war, all the rest having been constructed since 1948. James Ingodsby, working for the architects, Percy Thomas Partnership, Cardiff, has given advice on landscaping and one important section, linking the towering biology building with the more traditional Pantycelyn Hall, was laid out to suggestions made by Brenda Colvin, but in the main the two gardens reflect the ideas and preferences of the university staff. The Botany Garden was begun under the direction of the botany professor Lily Newton and then, after her retirement in 1958, by her successor Professor P.F. Wareing. He was joined in 1960 by Basil Fox who came from The Royal Botanic Garden, Edinburgh to be Curator of the Botany Garden at Aberystwyth. With such people in control it is not surprising that the emphasis in garden making around the University College of Wales has always been on plants and it is their range and the skill with which they have been used which give these two gardens their unique character.

Early on a nursery was established in the Botany Garden. This has had a considerable effect on the subsequent planting of both this garden and the college campus, since it has made it possible to propagate a large number of plants which are not available commercially and some of which are rarely, if ever, seen in other British gardens. Over the years it has also become apparent that home raised stock, accustomed from the outset to the soil and climate of the site, has a much greater chance of becoming established than plants imported from other localities and conditions. Even so only recently has it been found possible to plant semi-mature trees, so beloved of architects, and now only because of the rapidly increasing protection provided by trees and shrubs that were planted years ago while still young. Moreover in these early years it was essential to group plants densely for mutual protection and to encourage the canopy of foliage to rise uniformly.

Under these exposed conditions, or possibly because of the nature of the soil, autumn planting has proved unsuccessful, growth being excessively slow and the mortality rate high. March and April are the best planting months even for deciduous species though this might not hold true for places with a much lower rainfall than Aberystwyth.

Plas Penglais, the old mansion in the Botany Garden, is now the residence of the Principal and its immediate surrounds have been planned on fairly conventional lines but given distinction by some fine planting. There is a long raised terrace to one side of the house with parallel borders and a rectangular pool. In the shelter of the terrace wall great clumps of *Phormium colensoi* thrive and *Cornus capitata* flowers well in a protected corner at the end of the terrace. *Cytisus sessilifolius* is another good, but unfamiliar plant, notably light and graceful in habit and very free flowering. Around the house the terrace wall gives way to a more informal bank heavily planted with sun-loving shrubs and perennials including numerous species of cistus of which *Cistus palhinae* is the most decorative.

Osteospermums grow well here and it is interesting to note that a prostrate form of *Osteospermum ecklonis* has proved hardier than the more familiar bushy form. Below this bank the land falls away and is treated as open parkland with well-mown grass and specimen trees, the whole closed in by a belt of trees which almost completely conceals the new college buildings on the far side of the road.

That essential feature of any botanic garden, the order beds in which plants are grouped according to their families, is not planned in the regular rectangular beds familiar in old botanic gardens, but is filled with large island beds with sweeping lines which emphasise the flow of the land. The progression in planting illustrates a modern American theory of the evolutionary process and this has presented some problems for the gardeners since the more primitive orders are at the bottom of the slope, where the soil is relatively moist, and the more recent at the top, where it tends to be dry. Unfortunately this by no means always reflects the preferences of the plants themselves which may find themselves in highly uncongenial surroundings.

On the campus plants have been used with great skill and generosity to soften the outlines of uncompromisingly functional buildings and to retain the many steep banks which are an inevitable consequence of using a steeply sloping site for very large structures necessitating a great deal of excavation. Shrubs are often planted in bold groups of a kind and walls are allowed to 'jungle' with a riot of climbing plants or those shrubs which can readily be trained in such places. For the banks the prostrate forms of cotoneaster have proved particularly useful with *Cotoneaster microphyllus cochleatus* the best of them all.

A list has been prepared of about 500 plants which grow well and they are coded according to their degree of resistance to cold, wind and salt. In the top grade there are some surprising names, *Cassinia retorta*, among them, an almost unknown New Zealand evergreen which thrives at Aberystwyth. *Eucalyptus niphophyla* gets a higher rating than the more popular *E. gunnii* and *Senecio munroi* has proved far better than the oft recommended *S. rotundifolius*. My own 'best find' was an unusually compact and slow growing form of *Drimys winteri* which seems an ideal large-leaved evergreen for garden use. At Aberystwyth it appears to be regarded as the type form of the species but it is quite different from that which I have encountered in other gardens or grown myself. They make a speciality in the Botany Garden of obtaining seed of the same species from many different localities and these often reveal differences in habit and hardiness which could be invaluable to gardeners.

For those seeking a fast growing and hardy deciduous tree to replace the disappearing elms the Hungarian oak, *Quercus frainetta*, could well be the answer. It is growing splendidly in exposed positions in the campus and has just the right outline and leaf characteristics to blend perfectly into our landscape. The University College of Wales is full of such lessons for enterprising planters.

Opposite: Spring at Killerton

The Woodland Gardens

any of the new plant species coming into British gardens from foreign places did not so much require protection from cold as from hot and drying sunshine. Mainly these were the woodland and forest plants, and very prominent among them as the 19th century advanced were the rhododendrons from the Himalaya quickly to be supplemented by hundreds of new hybrids made by interbreeding them in gardens. Nearly all enjoy acid soils, a fair amount of atmospheric moisture and the kind of dappled shade given by fairly thin woodland in which both deciduous and evergreen trees are mixed.

Many of the gardens and parks made during the 18th century provided ideal conditions for rhododendrons and other shrubs from similar environments, and the British policy of planting coppices for shelter and amenity also fitted in very well with this new development in garden making. Like many other British innovations, woodland gardens were already in existence before they were labelled as such, and those who later wrote about them were wrongly credited with having invented a form of gardening which grew up spontaneously from the plant collectors' constant search for conditions that best suited whatever species were engaging their attention. It was a form of garden making that grew up without rules or any design theories and yet, probably because of the examples of pictorial composition which abounded in every country, most were planted with considerable taste and some have developed into masterpieces.

The Younger Botanic Garden

The road north from Dunoon skirts, for a few miles, the south-western shore of Holy Loch and then, at its head, turns east to cross the River Eachaig and then north again to enter the deep valley through which the river brings water from Loch Eck and the River Massan to the sea. In a little over a mile Glen Massan itself enters this main valley from the north east, and in the angle between the two, extending some way up the steep slopes of A 'Cruach, is Benmore, the loveliest spot in this very beautiful place. There are hills all around, many of them well over 1,500 feet high, though whether the summits of any will be visible depends upon the weather. For this is an area of high rainfall, 90 inches even in an average season, with moisture-laden air and frequent mist. The soil is acid and poor, leached by the rain. Yet, taken together, all these conditions suit perfectly many plants from the Himalayas and north-western America.

Until 1870 much of the valley was bare except for a little planting on the west side of Scots pine, European larch and Norway spruce which had been done some fifty years earlier. Then Mr James Duncan bought Benmore House and began to plant trees on a vast scale. In three years he is said to have put in 6.5 million trees, and these were destined to change the whole character of the place. Among them were many exotic kinds clearly chosen for their beauty or scientific interest rather than for any economic reason, and so Benmore developed into an arboretum of considerable merit. How long Mr Duncan continued to plant and enjoy the fruits of his labours I do not know, but by 1928 the arboretum belonged to Mr Harry George Younger, who gave it, in that year, to the nation.

Much of it was taken over by the Forestry Commission, which was naturally keenly interested in the varied collection of mature trees as well as in the possibilities of the site for further experiment. The mansion itself was acquired by Edinburgh Corporation as an adventure playground, and it would be hard to imagine a more exciting place for children brought up in a great city with little opportunity to explore wild country.

The remaining 100 acres was given to the Royal Botanic Garden, Edinburgh, which urgently needed just such a place for cultivation of trees and shrubs requiring much higher humidity and soil moisture than Edinburgh could supply. The great Edinburgh programme of research into the taxonomy of the rhododendron family was getting into its stride and conditions at Benmore were ideal for rhododendrons and azaleas. It was also highly desirable to extend considerably the collections of conifers and of some other trees and shrubs.

A bronze fountain in a semi-wild setting in the Younger Botanic Garden

Right: Hostas and candelabra primulas edge a narrow path at Benmore

So the Younger Botanic Garden came into being, a very large garden considered in its own right yet a relatively small part of the original estate which Mr Duncan had started to plant with such energy and imagination nearly 60 years before. The house stands in the garden but is not open to visitors, who do not enter by the Golden Gates in Glen Massan to the west but come in from the east and the Dunoon road, crossing once again the River Eachaig, this time on a wooden footbridge, and immediately entering one of the finest avenues of wellingtonias in Britain. These giant sequoiadendrons line the drive leading towards the house for something like 300 yards and average 130 feet in height, a truly impressive sight. When measured in 1970 the tallest trees exceeded 144 feet.

Much of the botanic garden lies to the north and north-east of this great avenue and is divided into several fairly well-defined areas. First there is an extensive pinetum in which the trees are sufficiently widely spaced to allow generous underplanting with rhododendrons and many other shrubs. At one end there is a small lake, its banks densely planted with moisture-loving shrubs and perennials. Here the visitor will encounter the first of several bronze statuary fountains which somewhat surprisingly decorate this mainly rather wild place.

Nevertheless all the designing at Benmore has not been contrived to look as if it had occurred naturally. Next to the pinetum is a large rectangular area which is entirely formal in conception. It is enclosed on three sides by walls or hedges but is open on the fourth, western side to the mountain slope. Paths run around it and also bisect it in both directions, and it is overlooked by an attractively-designed pavilion, the centrepiece of many of the most popular pictures of Benmore.

A third area extends for some distance up the mountainside, and here all possible steps have been taken to preserve the illusion of natural growth. Narrow paths wind up the slopes and can scarcely be seen because of the dense jungle of growth which envelopes them. Tall evergreen conifers give some protection to the north, but this is still a very exposed place in which plants must fight for their existence. When I first visited Benmore in 1968, only a few months after a freak storm had swept across southern

Opposite: Rhododendrons cover a slope in the Younger Botanic Garden

71

Scotland doing great damage to property in Glasgow and forests in many places, all but the lowest part of the mountainside at Benmore was closed to visitors because of the trees which still lay across it in all directions. It was a terrible sight, but foresters were already busy clearing the fallen trees, and a couple of years later, when I came to Benmore again, it was hard to remember that there had been so recently such a scene of devastation in this beautiful place.

For at its flowery peak in May and early June this mountainside is undoubtedly the most spectacular part of Benmore; the scene that is shown on the railway posters, gay with rhododendrons, azaleas, embothriums, and other flowering shrubs. They are the plants that know how to cling to the soil between the rocks, anchoring themselves firmly against gales and revelling in the acid soil and moist air. The only drawback is that the very conditions which make this such a paradise for plants often make it difficult to view them, and even more to photograph them clearly. If you are lucky to strike a sunny and clear day you will be rewarded with a stupendous spectacle and lovely views across the valley and even as far south as Holy Loch. Only once have I had this good fortune, yet I have always been thrilled by Benmore, even in the rain.

View from Benmore across the valley of the River Eachaig

This, of course, is due in large measure to the wonderful trees it contains. The monkey puzzles (*Araucaria araucana*) there are the finest I know in any British garden. All are positively beautiful, not just curious, many with branches sweeping right down to the soil and all densely clothed with lush green leaves totally unlike the ungainly mops sitting on top of scraggy trunks that one so often sees. One of the finest specimens, east of the house, was about 60 feet high in 1970 and there are others nearly as big. On the other side of the house is what is said to be the tallest western hemlock (*Tsuga heterophylla*) in Britain, 157.5 feet high in 1970, and two others close by then measured 141 feet and 139 feet. One magnificent Douglas fir in Glen Massan, on the extreme west of the garden rather outside the area usually covered by visitors, was just over 160 feet high in 1969 and, so far as I know, only one taller specimen has been recorded in Britain, at Powis Castle in Wales, where a tree was measured in 1970 as 177 feet high. Two other specially notable trees in the Glen Massan area are a 131 feet *Abies concolor* and another, of its variety *lowiana*, nearly 138 feet high.

At Benmore many rhododendrons have naturalised themselves and regularly regenerate from self-sown seed. This is true not only of the common *Rhododendron ponticum*, which has become a weed in many parts of Scotland, but also of choice Himalayan species such as *R. thomsonii* and *R. campanulatum*.

In the formal garden there is an extensive collection of naturally dwarf conifers, most of them sports from species of normal size. Many are golden leaved or otherwise variegated and all are of considerable interest to garden owners who lack the space to grow full-size trees. Kalmias, eucryphias, enkianthus, pieris, leptospermums and skimmias enjoy the peculiar Benmore conditions just as much as rhododendrons, and on the south-facing wall of the formal garden is the finest specimen of *Berberidopsis corallina* I have seen in any British garden. This beautiful Chilean climber, which may be extinct in the wild, is known as the coral plant because its hanging clusters of small, globular flowers look like scarlet beads. Experts always advise a shady spot for it, but at Benmore it grows in full sun, perhaps because the sunlight there is never sufficiently strong or sustained to do harm.

Leonardslee

Considered as a style, woodland gardening was of varying success. Some gardens were created purely as collections and have never become anything else. Others were planned with greater care or were introduced into existing landscapes which determined their form and imposed their own unity upon them. Leonardslee, at Lower Beeding, West Sussex, enjoyed both advantages besides being a collection of exceptional richness and, as a result, it is now one of the finest woodland gardens to be found anywhere in the world.

It would be difficult to conceive a more perfect site, on both sides of a steep valley running north and south along the western edge of St

Overleaf: A walk through the woodland at Leonardslee.

Top right: Azaleas beside one of the hammer ponds

Leonard's Forest. Here trees have grown for centuries and at one time were used as fuel for iron smelting. To provide water power for this rural industry a string of lakes, known as hammer ponds, was created in the valley, but soon steam replaced water wheels and the ponds ceased to have any further industrial use.

The original house was replaced in 1855 by another, higher up on the western lip of the valley where it overlooks most of the 80 or more acres of garden, as well as a great deal of surrounding woodland. On a fine day one can see the South Downs 14 miles away.

This was more or less how things were when Sir Edmund Loder purchased the place in 1887. He had married shortly before and had made one attempt at gardening in Northamptonshire on unsatisfactory soil. At Leonardslee he found exactly what he was seeking – beautiful site, sheltered on the valley sides, and a reasonably good soil, lime free and able to retain moisture even in summer. He began to plant at once and continued energetically up to the time of his death in 1920. At no time did he seek any professional guidance, but he had numerous friends and relations who were equally enthusiastic about trees and shrubs.

Woodland gardening was much talked about at this period. William Robinson and Gertrude Jekyll were advocating it in books and articles, and it was undoubtedly one of the fashionable things to do. Yet it seems probable that Sir Edmund Loder derived his ideas for Leonardslee more from what he saw in the wild than from anything he read or heard. For his second love was big-game hunting with a special interest in the antelope family, and he made frequent journeys to India, Africa and Canada.

Sir Edmund was soon breeding rhododendrons as well as collecting them. In 1900 he made the first crosses in what were to prove his most famous hybrids between *Rhododendron griffithianum*, a rather tender Chinese species notable for the size of its mainly white flowers, and *R. fortunei*, also from China but fully hardy and with smaller, shapely pink and fragrant flowers. He chose the best available forms of each species and

75

made the crosses both ways, once with *R. griffithianum* as the seed-bearing parent and twice with *R. fortunei* in this role. It was this latter method that gave the best results. The first flowers came in 1907 and the new hybrids were collectively named *R. loderi* in honour of their creator. The best combined the flower size of one parent with a good deal of the hardiness of the other. The colour range was from white to shell pink and most of the flowers were also sweetly scented.

But it was not simply rhododendrons and azaleas that were being planted in thousands in the Leonardslee valley. Large numbers of other trees and shrubs were also introduced, hardwoods and conifers, deciduous species and evergreens from many parts of the globe. There is an excellent guidebook to Leonardslee which reads like the catalogue of a notable botanic garden, so numerous are the names of rare or specially fine plants that it contains.

Quite separate from the woodland landscape, on the opposite side of the entrance drive close to what is now the visitors car park, Sir Edmund Loder made a large rock garden using local Sussex sandstone. It is a fine piece of work with paths winding between high-banked soil from which the rock appears as if outcropping in natural strata. Old photographs show it planted with many rock plants as well as with dwarf shrubs but nowadays for the sake of economy in upkeep, shrubs have been allowed to take over almost completely. Evergreen azaleas are particularly good here, some of them very old plants grown to considerable size yet still in good health and flowering freely each May.

In 1920 Sir Edmund died and the impetus for garden creation died with him. The place continued to be well maintained by his daughter-in-law but her main interest was cattle and she devoted much time to breeding Red Polls and Dexters. During the war the major part of the house was used as an officers' mess by the Canadian army, and no gardeners were employed. By the time Sir Giles Loder, grandson of Sir Edmund, took control in 1946 the garden was almost completely derelict, with grass waist high and all paths overgrown. It was doubtful how much could be saved, but Sir Giles and Lady Loder, both enthusiastic gardeners, determined to set all else aside and devote themselves to the garden.

I first visited Leonardslee in 1950 to obtain photographs for an article by Sir Giles which was to appear the following April in *Gardening Illustrated*. No one told me about the years of neglect and I saw nothing, nor do the pictures reveal anything now that I re-examine them, to give evidence of it. The lawns were trim, the paths excellent, the rhododendrons and azaleas full of bloom – so full that I was completely dazzled by them and failed to observe what a very well-designed garden Leonardslee is. Since the garden is normally open to the public only in late spring, when it is in full bloom, and some weekends in autumn, when the foliage colour is almost equally mesmeric, it may well be that other visitors have missed the point that this is a supremely beautiful woodland landscape, a work of art just as satisfactory when it is without exotic colour as when it is filled with it. Partly this is due to the nature of the site but equally it is clear that a great deal of thought has been put into the placing of new plants and the control of old ones or those which appear freely by self regeneration.

Statue of a boy and girl at Leonardslee

Sometimes it is necessary to cut shrubs almost to ground level and let them shoot up again to prevent lovely vistas being blocked with growth. This happens in places such as Mossy Ghyl, a narrow side valley which brings a stream down into the main channel. From the opposite side, and particularly from open spaces around the house, one can look down into this delightful place and the owners take every care that the view remains unspoiled. In one place there is a touch of formality to preserve and embellish a specially important vista. There is little waterfall which can be seen from the house and terrace and it is backed by solid blocks of clipped evergreens around which are tall conifers. In May and early June the place is filled with the brilliant colour of deciduous azaleas, but at any other season the silver streak of water seen against a dark green background is equally effective.

Sir Giles and Lady Loder have made many additions to Leonardslee. They have planted great numbers of new rhododendrons, azaleas and other shrubs, and an entirely new camellia grove in which there are several hundred camellias including the best of the new *Camellia williamsii* and *C. sasanqua* varieties. They have also erected two large unheated greenhouses for camellias and a third even larger house for a mixed collection of trees, shrubs and herbaceous perennials.

Another new feature that could be of great interest to owners of small gardens is a collection of dwarf conifers interplanted with small rhododendrons, a combination that is unusual but most successful.

Near the head of Mossy Ghyl a Coronation Garden has been made to commemorate the coronation of the Queen. This is a cleared glade surrounded by the best forms of *Rhododendron loderi*. The path to it leads through a fine collection of Asiatic magnolias flanked by massed azaleas.

Winter at Leonardslee. View of the South Downs from the top lawn

Any garden made primarily with plants grown in a natural manner is in a constant state of change. Old plants die out and new ones must be put in their places. Even more subtly plants grow and grow, almost imperceptibly changing the whole character of the garden. Owners of such gardens must for ever be making difficult decisions about these matters. Are valued plants to be restricted or removed? Are vistas of greater importance than the plants which tend to block them? Should replacement be done little by little so that it is as subtle as the changes which nature imposes or is it better to redevelop whole areas of a garden at one time? It is among the triumphs of Leonardslee that one is never conscious of any of these problems there. I have known the garden for many years and it has always looked right.

The Waterhouse and Isabella Plantations

When Charles I determined to develop the gardens at Hampton Court in the manner already fashionable on the Continent it became essential to find a water supply with sufficient head to operate the fountains he planned to instal. The Colne was selected, and a new artificial river was cut from Longford, eight miles away, to bring its waters to nearby Bushy Park. Here the Longford River filled a large reservoir from which the water was piped to Hampton Court. A little brick-built shed stands beside the reservoir, housing gear to control the flow of water, and so the reservoir came to be known as the Waterhouse Pond. Later two large coppices were planted in this part of Bushy Park, one immediately adjacent to the reservoir. In due time each acquired an undergrowth of rhododendrons, and walks were cut through the trees and bushes.

Water cascading into the woodland from the old reservoir in the Waterhouse Plantation

Streamside planting in the Isabella Plantation

But no one seems to have considered the possibility of these two little woodlands for really serious development until Mr J.M. Fisher was appointed Superintendent of Hampton Court gardens in 1949. By this time much of the surrounding fence had broken down and the Waterhouse Plantation was largely derelict and overgrown.

Mr Fisher immediately embarked on a programme of clearance and repair. The fences were replaced and the deer excluded. Old paths were reopened and widened and new ones made. A great deal of the old *Rhododendron ponticum* that formed the main undergrowth was removed to make way for better hybrids, particularly at this stage the fine hardy hybrids that had proved their garden worth.

Work continued steadily over the ensuing years, and was considerably accelerated from 1958 onwards when Mr Fisher was offered working parties from Wormwood Scrubs. The extra labour force extended into the second of the woodland plantations, so bringing a total of nearly 100 acres into the garden. In this second woodland there was a low and damp area which was flooded to form a fine lake with two islands.

Throughout the development Mr Fisher has shown a fine appreciation of design. He has had the advantage of an ample water supply and has used

One of the canals in the Waterhouse Plantation

it well. Some of the water courses are narrow and nearly straight, retaining much of their original ditch-like character. Others are wider and more winding, and some actually encircle areas of planting. In some places the water flows swiftly and in others appears almost motionless.

Water enters from the Waterhouse Pond beneath an old weeping willow which used to grow on the other side of the pond until it was towed to its present position. The water rushes down a cascade into the first of the new channels from which at one point it is actually piped under the Longford River to continue its function of filling the complex of streams and canals.

There is similar diversity in the treatment of the woodlands themselves. A few parts have been left dense, but most have been carefully thinned. There are completely open glades and other places where the trees have been left standing on close-mown grass with no underplanting to clutter the cloister-like appearance of their tall trunks.

The new plantings of rhododendrons, camellias and other shrubs are carefully disposed to channel long vistas through the glades and tree trunks. In many places daffodils are naturalised in the grass, together with native fern to follow the daffodils.

The streamsides have been liberally stocked with moisture-loving plants of all kinds, including primulas, rodgersias, hostas, astilbes and irises. On the higher ground, among the rhododendrons and azaleas, meconopses thrive so well that even *Meconopsis betonicifolia* attains a height of four feet.

In the second woodland there are many new conifers, some raised from seed obtained from Villa Taranto at Pallanza, Italy, where seed ripens well. Among these *Pinus montezumae*, now a good five feet tall, is looking remarkably happy in conditions that might be considered too cold and damp for it.

But this is by no means the only surprise in what are now usually referred to as the Woodland Gardens. They abound in good plants, most doing exceedingly well. *Parrotia persica* and *Parrotiopsis jacquemontiana* grow side by side. Large-leaved rhododendrons, including the creamy flowered *R. macabeanum*, are growing rapidly, unsinged by frost. *R. williamsianum* and other species and pedigree hybrids enjoy the shelter of the hardier hybrid rhododendrons. Swamp cypresses not unnaturally revel in the damp soil, and one, considerably older than the rest, has developed a particularly remarkable outcrop of 'knees' on its roots.

The Waterhouse Plantation is not the only post-war development of its kind with which Mr Fisher has been associated. At the time of his appointment to Hampton Court, Richmond Park also came under his care, and in 1950 he initiated a similar project there.

A little to the north of the road leading from the Robin Hood to the Kingston gates is an area of woodland known as the Isabella Plantation. It covers 42 acres and was planted about 1840 by Lord Sidmouth. The name probably commemorates a relation. Like the Waterhouse Plantation it remained a pleasant but unremarkable place until Mr Fisher determined to develop it.

The Isabella Plantation is on sloping land, contoured in two directions, with a little pool quite high on the slope and a small lake at the foot of it outside the area of trees. Despite two small lakes there is no generous water supply here and they were filled mainly by flood water.

Astilbe

In 1950 Mr Fisher began to clear the upper pool and to make a watercourse to the lake, but in the following year his connection with Richmond Park came to an end, and Mr George Thomson was appointed Superintendent there. He continued Mr Fisher's ideas on his own lines, so that the two gardens are now quite different in character.

An adequate water supply was obtained when the Metropolitan Water Board agreed to pump unfiltered Thames water to a reservoir in the plantation – as at Kew Gardens. Mr Thomson then proceeded to dig a second stream to the east of the first.

The overall plan in the Isabella Plantation is less complex than that at Bushy. Long open vistas have been preserved throughout the greater part of the length of both streams.

Both streams are well planted with primulas, calthas, astilbes, irises, hostas, ferns and other plants, but beyond the immediate area of the stream, the treatment is more restrained, many of the rhododendrons being planted as individual specimens. In this Mr Thomson was no doubt influenced by his early preference for species and first crosses between species, and during the years he had acquired many of the finest rhododendrons available from both the Exbury and Tower Court collections. But experience has led him to believe that, as close to London as Richmond is, hybrids are on the whole more reliable and make a better display than species, and now he is concentrating almost exclusively on the best of these. Some years ago Mr Richard Church wrote that these plantations were two of the most beautiful man-made scenes he had found. Time has increased their beauty and given them a feeling of peace and distinction at all seasons of the year.

Killerton

At Killerton one can study many of the predilections of 19th-century garden makers. It is often referred to as an arboretum and certainly successive generations of the Acland family who made it all seem to have had a great love for trees. But Killerton in Broad Clyst near Exeter is far more than that as any visitor can see. In front of the house there are extensive lawns beautifully laid out and maintained in the best English tradition. Specimen trees are dotted about on this smooth green carpet and there are large groups of rhododendrons and other shrubs to break it up still more. This informal approach finds a striking contrast in a long rectangular terrace or parterre which forms part of the southern boundary of the garden. It is not filled with bedding plants in season as one might expect but with a fine mixture of perennial plants, some woody, some herbaceous. Maybe this was not always so and that, in Victorian days, when labour was plentiful and coal was cheap these beds were planted with pelargoniums, heliotropes, marguerites and all the other bedding favourites but the present treatment certainly fits very well the central character of Killerton as a collector's garden.

When plant collection commenced at Killerton is by no means certain. Everyone seems to agree that the present house was built for the Aclands in 1778 though it has been extensively altered since. There is also consensus that it was the 10th baronet, Sir Thomas Acland, who first showed interest in the garden, the official National Trust guide saying that this was 'after the Napoleonic Wars', though it seems likely that he started considerably earlier. He certainly engaged John Veitch, a Scot, born in Jedburgh, to assist in the work and helped him to start a nursery, which Veitch called

Opposite: Killerton: the beech avenue

Right: Bluebell time at Killerton

Killerton Nursery, at Budlake. Miles Hadfield says, in 'Gardening in Britain', that the nursery was founded in 1808 and moved to Mount Rodford in 1832. These were the beginnings of the two great nursery firms of Veitch, one at Exeter the other at Chelsea, which were to play an important part in the introduction and distribution of plants from distant parts of the world. Between them they had much to do with the great increase in enthusiasm for plants in British gardens and Sir Thomas Acland, at Killerton, was probably the first to benefit from the Veitch genius.

To the north of terrace and lawns the land at Killerton rises steeply and at least two centuries ago someone planted an avenue of beeches across it. It is on this ridge that the major tree planting has always been carried out and continues to this day under the care of the National Trust, and the beech avenue has always been central to the very simple design. The main walk, gently zig-zagging up the steep incline, passes through the avenue with other narrower paths breaking from it to enable visitors to explore the collection in greater detail.

There are many trees at Killerton, some old, some new and because they have been planted over such a long period with little attempt to group them in a botanical way, the effect is extremely natural as if, in some strange way, trees from many different parts of the world had suddenly decided to grow in this lovely part of Devon. Whether by chance or design, visitors get frequent glimpses of the surrounding countryside framed by trees as

The Victorian summerhouse at Killerton

they ascend the hill. The summit is crowned by some of the tallest wellingtonias (*Sequoiadendron giganteum*) in the garden, their red trunks always torn by squirrels racing up and down them. Viewed from below they increase the apparent height of the hillside and form a skyline which can be identified from afar. In fact for those who dislike walking uphill and prefer woodland to individual trees, the finest views of Killerton are from below and especially from the terrace on its southern boundary.

At the western end of the lawns some other favourite Victorian features will be found. One is a charming thatched summer house with a couple of tiny rooms one of which has a floor made of sheeps' trotters. Beside this little building, which must have a favourite picnic place for generations of Acland children and their friends, is a cool and shady rock garden clearly never intended for alpine plants but just right for ferns, low growing herbaceous perennials and dwarf conifers.

Beneath the trees on the hillside there is a great deal of underplanting with rhododendrons, azaleas and other shrubs. In spring bluebells and daffodils grow in the grass and, where this is not too coarse, there are also crocuses and hardy cyclamens. Perhaps not all these existed in Acland days but the garden at Killerton does very clearly illustrate the eclectic taste of Victorian planters and their enthusiasm for the new trees and shrubs introduced from far off places.

Westonbirt Arboretum

While it was the Himalayan rhododendron that really set the 19th-century woodland gardens alight, it was the great coniferous trees from North-Western America that started the fashion for arboretums and pinetums as well as providing less specialised woodland with some of their most impressive trees. Robert Halford was one of the first private landowners to fall under their spell. At Westonbirt, Tetbury, Gloucestershire, he owned ample land to indulge his taste, much of it flat and nearly all with moderately acid soil capable of growing an exceptionally wide range of plants.

David Douglas made his first journey for the Horticultural Society to the Pacific Coast of North America in 1824 and continued his plant collecting there in successive expeditions until, in 1834, he fell into a pit dug as a trap for wild animals, and was killed by a bull already caught in it. Robert Halford began to plant his arboretum in 1829 and it would be nice to think that he was stimulated to do so by Douglas's introductions but that is unlikely, for it would have taken a longer period for even the first tree raised from Douglas's seed to be distributed at all widely. The true connection between the two events is that both are evidence of the rapidly increasing interest in trees which was to gather momentum as other collectors carried on the work, not only in the two Americas but also in Asia. It is significant that at Westonbirt the early years seem to have been spent mainly in establishing native trees and that it was not until the 1850's that exotics began to appear there in any number.

Robert Halford did not die until 1892, by which time all his early plantings were mature and he had long enjoyed the pleasure of owning a magnificent arboretum. His son, George, who was later knighted, was at least as enthusiastic as his father about trees and began planting at Westonbirt in 1875. When he died in 1920 Westonbirt was inherited by a nephew, the Earl of Morley, who also continued to plant trees until his death in 1951 when the arboretum was taken over by the Forestry Commission.

Because of this fortunate succession of ownership over more than a century, Westonbirt Arboretum has always been well cared for and has been, and still is, in a state of constant development. New plantations have been made and old ones renewed. Most important of all, new species and varieties have been added to the collection throughout its long life so that it is now probably the richest in variety of material in Britain. Yet there has never been any major alteration to Robert Halford's original plan though there have been many additions to it.

What Halford set out to do was to plant a woodland facing his home, Westonbirt House, but separated from it by the Bath to Tetbury road. He visualised it much on 17th-century lines with large blocks of trees separated by wide allées or 'rides' so placed that they would create long vistas from or towards the house. Other rides cut across these, so creating a grid effect though never actually parallel to one another or crossing at right angles.

When in later years the arboretum was extended far beyond sight of the house, geometry was abandoned in favour of free flowing lines with much narrower paths curling about among and around the trees. In plan it all looks very different; on the ground it matters far less for it is the trees which always dominate and design is of minor significance, not very obvious when viewed from eye level.

Though it was planned as an arboretum and is always referred to as such, Westonbirt has developed into something much more complex. It is now really a vast woodland garden in which trees predominate both in numbers and importance but with many other plants grown as undercover. Autumn has become a favourite season for visiting Westonbirt because of the magnificent colour of some of the ripening leaves, but the richest and most concentrated colour is always to be found in the Acer Glade, much of it coming from garden forms of Japanese maple which are large shrubs rather than trees. In late spring and early summer rhododendrons are in

Opposite: Autumn colour at Westonbirt

Right: The Acer Glade

bloom in some areas particularly within what is known as the Circular Drive (it is anything but circular) where the planting is reminiscent of that in Savill Gardens.

There is no doubt which is the most spectacular group of trees in Westonbirt Arboretum. It is situated midway along Halford Ride on its southern side where it borders on Acer Glade and it is composed of 20 trees of *Libocedrus decurrens*. This superb evergreen tree grows wild in Oregon and California where it is fairly variable in habit but in Britain it is always very narrow in proportion to its height. The trees at Westonbirt are now around 80 feet high yet barely 10 feet through and they are planted so closely that they rise side by side like a gigantic group of organ pipes. They are not as old as they might seem having been planted by Sir George Halford in 1910 but they are one of the unforgettable sights here and are not exceeded in dramatic effect by any similar group of trees I know in any British garden.

The Savill and Valley Gardens

When in 1932 Mr E.H. Savill, as he then was, began to make a small bog garden beside a little stream in Windsor Great Park he was launched on a project which was to grow far beyond his expectations. He was fortunate in engaging the interest of Prince Albert, later to become King George VI, and his wife, Elizabeth, who lived in Royal Lodge not far away. Both were keen gardeners and it was with their patronage and encouragement that this small undertaking began to grow into the greatest series of landscape gardens made in Britain since the first world war.

The creation of what is now known as the Savill Garden occupied the next eighteen years though little progress was made during the war. But by 1950 it was complete and had developed from the original wild garden into a much more complex design which embraced most of the features common to 20th-century large gardens. There were herbaceous borders and a formal rose garden, myriads of ornamental shrubs, including a fine collection of rhododendrons, several pools, peat beds, a number of raised rock beds, an alpine meadow and a large greenhouse. There had even been an attempt to give the garden a clearly defined starting point in the shape of a high wall to suggest some substantial property at hand to which this garden was an adornment. It was all done with great skill and imagination, the garden was an immense success when it was opened to the public.

But Sir Eric Savill was not content. He had tasted the excitement of garden making and wished for more of it. George VI was dead but Queen Elizabeth was willing to see the work continued and an ideal site existed about a mile to the south. It lay beyond the polo field on the northern shore of Virginia Water, a large lake which had been created 200 years earlier by the brothers Thomas and Paul Sandby as part of a scheme for improving Windsor Great Park in the then fashionable landscape manner and at the same time dealing with drainage problems that caused flooding in this part of the park after heavy rain.

The damp dell where the creation of the Savill Garden began

The site at Virginia Water was very different from that at the Savill Garden. Here ample water was already in existence, many fine trees were fully developed and a whole series of small valleys ran down to the lakeside. It was a 20th-century planter's dream site, ripe for further development with all the new and exciting trees and shrubs that had been introduced to Britain since the 18th century. Sir Eric Savill brought to this new development all the experience gained in his first venture.

The work proceeded gradually and continues to the present day. So far as I know there has never been any definite plan, no point at which these Valley Gardens, as they have come to be called, could be declared complete. One project has followed another as dictated by the nature of the site and the time and labour available.

First there was the Valley Garden itself, almost an 18th-century Arcadian landscape, a green valley sweeping down to the water in curves and gradients as smooth as any that Lancelot Brown could have devised and with quite restrained planting of exotic shrubs and colour mainly restricted to the rhododendron and azalea season in May and early June.

Hard by is Azalea Valley, with far less green and a great deal more colour, and on the other side the famous Punch Bowl, a horticultural *tour de force* which is admired or disliked according to one's taste in such things. Here in a natural amphitheatre, tens of thousands of evergreen azaleas, including many of the best of the Kurume varieties, are ranged in tiers like a brilliantly dressed audience at a stage show with blue, grey, and silvery conifers on the 'stage' below and many Japanese maples among azaleas to give renewed colour in the autumn. This remarkable garden reaches its peak display as May gives way to June.

There are many other fine things in the Valley Gardens; a hillside almost completely covered with dawn redwoods; a large and imaginatively planted heather garden in which many exotic birches merge with the heathers; orchard-like plantations of ornamental cherries; long vistas through conifers; multitudinous rowans including all the finest Asiatic species; further drifts of azaleas, some carefully segregated into colour groupings; fine specimens of various species of southern beech (nothofagus), and in some places dense underplanting with hydrangeas.

The catalogue of what is there can give no idea of the skill with which the planting has been done and the lovely scenic effects that have been created. The Valley Gardens have never attracted the publicity lavished on the Savill Garden, and, though constantly open, are much less accessible to the public since there is no nearby car park except on those days when polo is being played and cars are admitted to the park by the polo field. Otherwise one must walk from the Savill Garden, or trudge uphill from Wick Road or Virginia Water. All routes lead through delightful scenery and the journey is well worth while for it has always seemed to me that the Valley Gardens represent the peak of Sir Eric Savill's achievement in the handling of woody plants and are all the better for being wholly informal. Yet the two gardens do excellently complement each other for in the Savill Garden there are conditions to suit the herbaceous plants, many of which require a higher degree of maintenance than trees and shrubs. Here will be found all the best meconopsis species and hybrids, primulas galore, lilies, irises, lysichitums, astilbes, wood anemones, hostas, agapanthus and hundreds more with daffodils, crocuses and other bulbs naturalised in the grass and many choice alpine plants superbly grown in rock beds which are so much easier to manage and re-make periodically than conventional rock gardens. Between them the Savill and Valley Gardens provide an object lesson in all that is best in 20th-century garden making.

Right: The Valley Gardens: azaleas in flower in the Punch Bowl

Opposite: Raised rock beds beside a wall clothed with climbing plants in the Savill Garden

Gardens for Display

The vast industrial expansion of the 19th century had profound effects on the art and craft of gardening. Great wealth was generated and much of it was concentrated in the hands of financiers and industrialists some of whom were anxious to establish their new found importance by building themselves mansions and laying out fine grounds around them. Some followed traditional styles and a few, as we have seen, became fascinated by plants and laid the foundations of great collections. But for a majority conspicuous display was a more immediate, if less publicised, consideration and much of the new horticultural technology was perfectly adapted to this end. Rapid improvement in the construction and heating of glasshouses made it possible to propagate plants far more easily and rapidly. Many of the new exotic plants which were too tender to survive outdoors, even in the mildest parts of Britain, could, nevertheless, be planted in the open throughout the summer, and since many of them, because of their tropical origin, were accustomed to flower non-stop for many months, they were admirably adapted for the purpose of making a great show of colour. To the species were quickly added new hybrids, some so different from their parents that they were virtually new, man-made species. Whole new races of pelargoniums, dahlias, begonias and roses came into existence and other plants such as lobelias, heliotropes, verbenas, stocks and marguerites were greatly improved in flower quality and increased in colour range.

These plants fitted well into a style of gardening which had previously been confined almost exclusively to the palace gardens of kings and princes in which planting schemes could be varied frequently, in extreme cases, such as for Louis XIV at Versailles, every few days. Bedding out was the term now applied to this method of planting for which relays of plants were reared in greenhouses and frames to be planted out in special display beds in the garden in successive batches as they came into flower or produced their most colourful foliage. These plants were usually massed to produce great sheets of colour, often used to create intricate patterns within the overall pattern by the often elaborate geometrical shapes of the beds themselves.

To accommodate this craze for bedding out as well as to satisfy the architects' demand for order and balance, at any rate in the immediate surroundings of the mansions, terraces, which had been anathema to the 18th-century landscapes, came back into fashion. By the middle of the 19th century they were being made everywhere, sometimes in the most unlikely places. Sir Joseph Paxton was designing terraces to overlook Humphry Repton's landscape at Tatton Park, Sir Charles Barry was engaged on terraces for Lancelot Brown's landscape at Harewood House and other gardens by Brown were being similarly embellished. At Trentham Park W.A. Nesfield was called in to provide designs which would convert the whole of the area between the lake and mansion into a series of huge terraces with a quite bewildering array of flower beds for vast spring and summer displays. The mansion has disappeared, destroyed by fire, but the terraces and the bedding out remain, preserved in an age of less conspicuous private wealth by being converted for use as a public amusement park. At about the same time George Kennedy, also connected with Drummond Castle, was providing Lord Lambourne with more discrete plans for terraces to 'improve' Brown's lovely landscape at Bowood.

This is the style of garden making which is popularly regarded as 'Victorian' though it had started well before Queen Victoria came to the throne and continued *for several decades after her death. It is still the favourite gardening style for most municipal parks but its high cost, both in terms of actual money and of labour, has long since made it impracticable for most privately owned gardens except on a very restricted scale. Oddly enough it remains the most popular and widely admired mode of planting for small town gardens and is the style that usually monopolises most of the prizes when competitions are held in towns or housing estates to encourage garden making.*

In its favour this method of gardening permits a greater continuity of colour than any other and in the wholly man-made environment of a town or a muncipal park it can look entirely in place. Against it must be recorded an early descent into vulgarity aided by the use of vivid colour contrasts to attract attention. It is an odd result of this particular fashion in garden making that plant breeders now spend a vast amount of effort and skill in producing plants that can be raised from seed and yet remain virtually identical in habit and colour so that they can be produced cheaply and then be massed in beds without there being a single one which by some tiny feature of individuality distracts the eye. It would seem that money and time might be spent on more worthwhile projects.

Even roses have not escaped for when, towards the close of the 19th century, they were, by interbreeding with tea varieties, induced to flower most of the summer they, too, were dragged into the display gardens as semi-permanent occupants which would reduce, by a little, some of the cost of seasonal bedding-out. Rose gardens proliferated as had Italianate terraces a generation or so earlier and they, too, were made formal and exclusive of other plants. The demand was for varieties that would flower ever more freely, more continuously and at a more even height so that the required level sheets of uninterrupted colour could be produced. As usual the public got what it wanted. Roses lost their individuality and grace, became flat-topped bushes requiring hard pruning and heavy feeding to keep them in condition and lost their reputation as free flowering shrubs which were good companions for many other kinds of plant. It is a belief that still lingers and is, to some degree, true of many 'bedding' varieties of rose. But now the pendulum of fashion is swinging once again and there is increasing demand for 'shrub' roses (as if roses were ever anything else than shrubs) which can be used in all manner of way in gardens including in mixed plantations of shrubs, herbaceous perennials, annuals and bedding plants.

Not many of the 'gardens for display' were conceived solely in these terms. Often they were additions to existing landscape gardens and the new terraces, as well as providing a more appropriately architectural surround for the house, were also convenient platforms from which the landscaped vistas could be enjoyed. Even in new properties there was usually a progression from the display methods of gardening near the house to less formal glade and woodlands in the outer reaches. Occasionally this logical progression was reversed and formal and informal styles were mixed without obvious reason, and there have been frequent occasions when gardens, or features in gardens, originally designed for display have been altered, usually very successfully, to meet the demands of a poorer and less ostentatious generation.

Opposite: The statue of Venus by the half-moon pond at Hever Castle flanked by beds of 'Rosemary Rose'

Drummond Castle

Though the garden of Drummond Castle does not belong to the great 17th-century period of garden making it does reveal, to a superlative degree, all the twists, quirks and embellishments that were applied to that tradition when it was resurrected two centuries later during the great revolt from the flowerless gardens of the landscape era. Opinions differ as to the exact date at which the great parterre at Drummond Castle was first laid out. Most probably it was altered several times even in its first two or three decades and without doubt it has been modified in our own times partly to heal the ravages of two wars but also to make it manageable under conditions of ever rising costs and chronic shortage of labour willing to remain in private employ. For Drummond Castle is still privately owned by the Earl of Ancaster and maintained primarily for his pleasure though it is open to the public quite frequently from April to the middle of August.

This great parterre is one of the major garden spectacles of Britain : a vast formal design that displays itself with the self assurance of a Vaux-le-Vicomte or Versailles, though it lacks the subtlety of Vaux and has none of the hidden features that make those Le Nôtre masterpieces such fascinating places to explore. Yet if the garden of Drummond Castle does reveal itself rather too quickly and completely, it delays that revelation until the very last moment, and until the spectator has reached the vantage point from which the garden makes its most powerful impact. It owes this dramatic quality to its situation in a valley, screened from view by both the ancient castle and the more modern house.

The main entrance to Drummond Castle is a mile away to the east on the road from Crieff to Muthill. The drive passes through a rather narrow avenue of hardwood trees, mainly lime and beech, flanked by woodland and farmland, the effect being rural rather than grand. Visitors to the

The keep and house of Drummond Castle viewed from the parterre

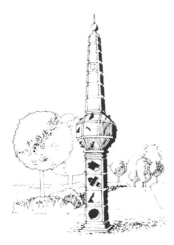

The multiplex sundial in the centre of the parterre

garden continue along this drive, past the north face of both house and castle, which on this side are rather stark and forbidding, unrelieved by any vestige of garden.

Entering an outer courtyard, one continues through the archway of the old keep, all that remains of the 15th-century castle, into an inner courtyard paved with roughly dressed sets which separates the keep from the west (and most recent) wing of the house. Still there is no sign of the garden, which remains hidden by a low wall to the right and the very considerable drop in level on this side.

The castle and house are, in fact, built on the crest of a rocky outcrop, and the garden is made in terraces on the steep south side of this ridge and on the floor of the valley below. Crossing the inner courtyard, one emerges on the uppermost terrace at the head of a great stairway leading down to the valley and also giving access to the lower terraces.

What is immediately revealed is a parterre over 13 acres in extent laid out on the slightly undulating floor of the valley in the form of a St Andrew's Cross with three parallel paths across it and more intricate patterns worked in between the main lines of the design.

The narrow but deep terraces on the north side of the valley are ornamented with stone balustrades, statues and busts. The stairway is also of stone, handsomely balustraded and ornamented, now dividing, now rejoining, and at one point passing over and around a large water basin in a shell-like recess.

The main pattern of the parterre is made with turf, gravel and plant beds, with the more intricate features drawn in edging box and larger hedges of beech. In summer there are great diagonal bands of silver and grey, provided by *Anaphalis triplinervis* and *Senecio laxifolius*, and some of the details are filled in with the blues and lavenders of violas, the white of roses and the orange and gold of marigolds.

But flower colour is now always subsidiary to that of foliage, though it was not always so. There are a great many topiary specimens, mainly cut from yew, holly, and Portugal laurel, but with other trees and shrubs for greater variety: some green, some bronze and some golden. The shapes are mostly simple, columns, cones and mushrooms predominating and they vary greatly in size. Mixed with them are numerous purple-leaved trees, Japanese maples, purple plums, a fine copper beech planted by Queen Victoria in 1842, and there is also one large golden elm.

There are numerous statues, urns and other architectural features, including several arches and a portico in classical style. Most remarkable of these is the tall sundial that occupies the central position in the parterre. This bears the date 1630, is in the form of an obelisk and has something like 50 separate faces. It is said to have been designed and made by John Mylne, Master Mason to Charles I, and to have been commissioned by John Drummond, 2nd Earl of Perth, especially for Drummond Castle.

The parterre is bounded to the west by a beech hedge beyond which is parkland, to the east by a multi-arched stone bridge across a small lake with more fine trees, around and to the south by the 9-feet high wall of the kitchen garden. Beyond this is the little Drummond Burn, and then the south side of the valley, rising more gently than the north, is well planted

The great parterre at Drummond Castle

with a good collection of evergreen and deciduous trees through the middle of which there is a wide grass ride. Half way up this open space a large statue of Dagon serves as an eye-catcher, if one were really needed in a design so boldly executed as this.

It might be supposed that the history of so remarkable a garden would be well recorded, but in Britain, where gardens tend to be made and re-made over long periods, largely by amateurs and their own employees, this is seldom so, and Drummond Castle is no exception. Accounts of its origin and development differ greatly, and except as they relate to the last 100 years or so must be regarded as unreliable.

Some state that the parterre was created in the mid-17th century by the 2nd Earl of Perth and that he placed the sundial where it stands today. But a large-scale survey prepared by John Knox in 1810 gives no indication of any parterre, though it does clearly show the 3-acre kitchen garden laid out in rectangles very much as it is today, and seems also to indicate a terrace on the north slope.

Nor is there any sign of the parterre in a drawing of Drummond Castle made by John Claude Nattes in 1799 and published in a book of engravings by James Fittler in 1804. This shows castle and house from the south east and depicts a muddy lane, a rather unkempt hedge and what appears to be a meadow. The brief account of the place accompanying this print states that the house commands a magnificent view over Strathearn and only wants water to make it very picturesque – hardly a term any 18th-century writer would use for a formal design.

A few years later Dr John Macculloch, in one of his letters to Sir Walter Scott (published in Highlands and Western Islands of Scotland, 1824) also praises the magnificence of the site, but goes on to describe the grounds as 'a wilderness from which even the owners are excluded . . . Art might accomplish in a few brief years all which is here demanded and render Drummond Castle the pride of the Lowlands and the third jewel, at least, of Scotland.'

They were prophetic words. By 1822, before Macculloch's comments had been published, J.C. Loudon was recording in his Encyclopaedia of Gardening that Drummond Castle had been greatly enlarged and its grounds extended and highly improved by Lord Gwydyr 'assisted by his ingenious steward, Lewis Kennedy'. This was one of the sons of John Kennedy, partner in the famous Hammersmith nursery firm Lee and Kennedy. Lewis appears to have gone to Drummond Castle about 1818, the year in which his father dissolved his partnership with James Lee, leaving the latter in sole command of the nursery. Records at Drummond Castle suggest that Lewis Kennedy was still there in 1860, so he must have been intimately connected with all the improvements that were made during that period.

The handsome wrought iron gates for the entrance to the drive were obtained from Italy in 1825, and many of the statues also came from Italy though possibly at a later date. The 1865 Ordnance Survey shows the parterre more or less as it is today, and it is depicted in much greater detail in a 'Plan of Garden with Alterations and Improvements since 1838', which is signed George P. Kennedy, Architect.

Whether he designed the great parterre at Drummond Castle or was merely recording what was already there is not clear, but either way the date 1838 must have some special significance. It seems not unreasonable to regard it as the starting date for the parterre, in which case Queen Victoria's ceremonial tree planting in 1842 may well have celebrated its completion.

Nineteenth-century pictures and accounts agree in depicting the parterre planted all over, mainly with shrubs and herbaceous plants. Blocks of rhododendrons, Portugal laurels and azaleas filled some of the areas that are now grass or gravel, and herbaceous borders lined the diagonals of the cross and ran along the foot of the terraces. The effect of such dense planting was to obscure the design, but now, with the greatly simplified planting mode essential by present-day economics, the pattern is fully revealed as, no doubt, was the original intention.

The planting of the terraces and the steep banks between them has also been changed. Where once were roses and later clipped laurels there is now a bold pattern (it might be likened to that of a Scottish stocking top) composed of large blocks of shrubs. This was prepared by Mr L.R. Russell, of Richmond Nurseries, Windlesham, and includes blocks of heathers, brooms, shrubby potentillas, prostrate junipers and other low-growing shrubs.

Sutton Park

Percy S. Cane, who died in 1976 after working for more than 70 years as a landscape architect, was not one of those who thought much of bedding plants and so it may seem strange to include one of his gardens in a chapter on Gardens for Display. Yet he did carry on the Victorian tradition of terrace building and often his terraces were gaily planted, though more

The new garden of Sutton Park looking out over the old landscaped park

likely with herbaceous perennials or roses than with plants that needed to be replaced several times a year.

He had very strong views on design and though the garden at Sutton Park, Sutton-on-Forest, North Yorkshire is certainly not one of his greatest achievements (he only appears to have visited it a few times to prepare outline plans and suggestions for planting) it was done towards the close of his active career and might well be used as a textbook illustration for many of the Cane maxims. Was it not he who stated with his usual positiveness that a pool in shade was a depressing object and that, if it contained a fountain, it must be in sunlight? Well that point is well demonstrated at Sutton Park as are his views that if an area is large, it must be divided into several gardens each with its individual character yet each happily related to its neighbour. He was also fond of pointing out that a sense of outdoor proportions, so essential in designing a garden, was quite different from that necessary when planning a house, and he had also in one of his numerous books on garden design called attention to the way in which the straight low line of a wall can heighten the beauty of scenery beyond.

All these dicta and many more Cane ideas will be found expressed at Sutton Park. The house is Georgian, built of mellow brown brick with a central block and two matching wings. The architect was Thomas Atkinson, and the main block was completed about 1728 with the wings being added 10 or 12 years later. It stands in the village of Sutton-on-Forest, too close to the main street to permit much garden making on that side, but to the south, where the land falls from the house the view across the countryside is completely unobstructed. The park is reputed to be by Capability Brown, but there does not appear to be any firm evidence for this and from the rather regular size and disposition of the tree clumps and the absence of any considerable sheet of water I would assume it to be by some lesser 18th-century landscapist.

The garden on the south side, overlooking this park, consists of three linked terraces flanked by considerable areas of lawn with island beds and glades leading, on the east side, to a woodland garden and a little temple nearly half a mile away. Only the first two styles were suggested by Mr Cane, the woodland walk being a happy addition of the owners, Major and Mrs Reginald Sheffield who came to live at Sutton Park in 1962.

The terraces are roughly equal in size but different in design and planting. The first has large rectangular areas of turf with smaller panels set in the paving beside the house. Flowers are restricted to the perimeter, but here they are used lavishly, especially in wide borders against the house and above the retaining wall. There are roses in plenty, many fuchsias, flowering shrubs, herbaceous perennials and climbers. The colour scheme is restricted, with blues, greys and white predominating, but also quite a lot of pink mainly from the roses and fuchsias. The roses are largely old fashioned and shrub varieties such as 'Maiden's Blush', 'William Lobb', 'Buff Beauty' and 'Lavender Lassie' with 'Chaplin's Pink Climber' smothering two light metal arbours, one on each wing, and 'Félicité et Perpétue' sharing the house wall with jasmine, wisteria and other climbers. More wisterias, trained as standards find a place in the terrace border.

Opposite: Well-planted flower borders at Sutton Park

A statue amongst the flowers

Stone stairs, their balustrades clothed in vines and white wisteria, and further decorated with flower-filled urns, lead down to the second terrace which was planned as a rose garden but is now used for many other flowers, though roses still predominate. It consists of a lawn broken by two matching groups of beds, each forming a rectangle. It was Mr Cane's intention to pave these areas, using the grass only as a surround, which would certainly have emphasised the pattern, but the change to an all over cover of grass undoubtedly gives a softer, more restful effect.

Again the colour scheme is restricted, but there is more pink here with 'Blessings' and 'Prima Ballerina' prominent among the roses. These roses share their beds with pinks and other flowers and some of the beds have been completely given over to perennials and shrubs with the grey willow-leaved pear a feature in some. But the most exciting planting here is in the side border beneath the terrace wall where shrubs and perennials grow up to mingle with those on the terrace above, creating the effect of one uninterrupted bank of bloom with the masonry almost completely screened. Here there are lilacs, philadelphus, buddleias, echinops, delphiniums and many more, with lots of grey-leaved plants such as lavender, lavender cotton, artemisias and *Senecio greyi*. In the middle of this mass of bloom Mrs Sheffield has placed a statue on a pedestal at just the right height to create the illusion that the female figure is walking on the flowers.

As seen from the house the third terrace is a green parterre of grass, broken only by the water which could be described as a canal pool were not the simple elongated rectangle broken by a semicircular bulge on the south side to match the curve of a rotunda beyond, formed by the boundary hedge of close-trimmed beech. One of the best views of the house is from the heavy stone seat which fits snugly into this alcove. Plants pour over into this terrace along the balustrades of the steps, but otherwise there is little planting in the immediate line of vision, the terrace wall being clearly revealed and strongly vertical lines added to it by a row of regularly spaced columnar conifers. There are also urns for flowers, one at each corner of the pool, and two of a more elaborate design equally spaced between pool and terrace wall and raised on stone pedestals for greater emphasis. The pool has a fountain and a few discreet pads of water lilies, but no marginal plants to blur the definition of the paved edges. Only a rose 'Wedding Day', spilling out of a cedar tree, breaks the formality of this section – but this really belongs to another story.

For if, instead of looking back over the terraces, one turns to left or right, a completely different picture is revealed. Now the bottom terrace is seen to merge into lawns broken into flowing curves and glades by irregular island beds or by being permitted to penetrate into the embracing woodland. Yet though the outlines are now freehand rather than geometrical, planting remains as carefully studied as before.

Foxgloves are used freely, but they are all of an unusual apricot variety. There are mulleins, giant seakale (*Crambe cordifolia*) lady's mantle, cardoons, bergenias and many more to give an almost complete cover to the cultivated soil, but the verges are kept clean and sharp so that the shapes show clearly. It is as though the gardener wished to indicate that, while accepting hints from nature, he was not willing for her to take command.

Arley Hall

So widespread is the belief that William Robinson invented the herbaceous border in the last quarter of the 19th century that it is fascinating to discover a splendid pair of borders created a good quarter century before Robinson came on the scene. They are at Arley Hall near Northwich, Cheshire, and they were first depicted in a plan of the garden dated 1846. Later watercolour paintings and early photographs show them much as they are today, the principal change being that they are now separated by mown turf and not, as formerly, by a wide gravel path with grass verges.

They are very large borders, 250 feet long and something like 50 feet wide including the central walk, and they lead to a stone pavilion or garden room known as the Alcove. On one side they are backed by a tall, buttressed hedge of yew, on the other by a high wall with matching yew buttresses and lower hedges with topiary ornamentation wrap around the end.

Arley and its surrounding farm lands have belonged to the Warburton family for centuries, though inheritance has not always been by the direct male line. The present house, in neo-Jacobean style, was built by Rowland Egerton to whom the property came when his great uncle, Sir Peter Warburton, died childless, whereupon he added Warburton to his name. Rowland Eyles Egerton-Warburton began to build a new house in the 1830s. He employed a local architect named George Latham, but dominated the whole undertaking himself, deluging the architect with

Overleaf: The twin herbaceous border and the pavilion or 'Alcove' at Arley Hall. Bottom right: The sunken Fish Garden at Arley Hall

Below: The Ilex Avenue at Arley Hall

numerous suggestions, often in the form of detailed drawings, for he had considerable architectural knowledge. Work went on intermittently for something like 30 years, and it was over a similar period that the garden was created. It is possible that Latham may also have supervised the construction of this, at least in its more architectural aspects, but there is little doubt that it was the owner who determined its shape and style and controlled the planting.

Though garden and house are adjacent, the one is not designed as a setting for the other. Instead the main prospect from Arley Hall is south-wards over parkland, much as it must have been for the 18th-century mansion which preceded it. The new garden, which lies to the west, is about eight acres in extent, broadly wedge shaped with its apex resting on the forecourt of the hall. A very large and ancient tithe barn, which straddles the entrance drive, also projects into the garden and one of Rowland Warburton's 'improvements' was to surmount this tithe barn with an elaborate Bavarian-style clock tower, which looks rather odd from some angles, but is undeniably effective seen head-on down the tall avenue of pleached limes which line the drive.

The garden is entered from the forecourt through handsome wrought-iron gates which contribute to its separateness. Immediately ahead is a long straight terrace, the Furlong Walk, following the south-eastern boundary of the garden which is separated from the park only by a sunk wall and ha-ha. At the far end a few steps lead down into a circle, a kind of belvedere, backed by shrubs, ringed with roses, but which on the south is also completely open to the park.

From this key point a shorter avenue, lined by enormous drum-shaped columns of clipped holm oak and therefore known as the Ilex Avenue, leads due north into a very large walled garden which was certainly in existence in the 18th century. It is known that these holm oaks were planted about 1840 when they probably formed the main feature of Rowland Warburton's new garden, deliberately centred on the long axis of the old walled kitchen garden.

The tithe barn surmounted by
the Bavarian-style clock

The twin herbaceous borders run parallel with the south wall of this old kitchen garden, crossing the Ilex Avenue at right angles. Since they were in existence in 1846 it would seem reasonable to regard them as Rowland Warburton's second great stroke of design; the Furlong Walk, said to have been made in 1856, being the third. This was doubtless intended to emphasise the existing line of the boundary and complete a large right-angled triangle with its hypotenuse extended to the forecourt of the house.

Meantime he had presumably been filling in the intervening space with plants and other features, some of which remain although a few have disappeared. Among the survivals is a romantic little tea cottage tucked in to the south of the herbaceous borders almost where they join the Furlong Walk, though the two are hidden from one another by the high yew hedge which provides shelter and seclusion for both. Originally the tea house overlooked a formal parterre which an early engraving shows filled with circular beds and bedding plants. When hybrid tea roses came into fashion late in the century this became a rose garden, and in 1904 in 'Some English

Gardens' Gertrude Jekyll described it as having 'beds concentrically arranged leaving spandrels of beds of other shapes', which is more or less the way it remained until 1960.

Beyond the Ilex Avenue to the west the Warburtons made a semi-wild rock and water garden which is still there and is known as the Rootree. Miss Jekyll describes a maze at the back of the Alcove and a bowling green reached by an archway cut in the yew hedge near the Alcove. The maze has disappeared and the bowling green has become a tennis court, but between it and the Rootree is a little sunken garden with central pool and numerous trim columns of cypress, which give the effect of topiary columns without the labour of clipping. It is known as the Fish Garden, and was added sometime between the two wars.

But the most important alterations at Arley Hall have been made in the last 16 years by Viscountess Ashbrook, a great granddaughter of Rowland Egerton-Warburton. She had the advice of James Russell in this work. First she took in hand the rose garden, which was not very satisfactory since hybrid-tea roses have never done very well at Arley Hall. By contrast many old-fashioned and shrub roses grow splendidly. So she swept away the fussy little formal beds and replaced them with large sweeping borders which are now completely filled with a glorious array of roses grown with a minimum of pruning and a maximum licence to spread and sprawl as nature intended.

Even greater alterations were made to the walled garden, which completely transformed the character of this very large enclosure. For centuries it had been the main source of supply of fruit and vegetables for the residents at Arley, but, as so often happened in old kitchen gardens, it combined ornament with utility. After the last war it was developed on more commercial lines and the old flower borders and trained fruit trees were removed. As labour costs rose this venture proved increasingly unprofitable and eventually fruit and vegetables were confined to a smaller, adjacent enclosure and the original kitchen garden was planned and planted solely for ornament. The walls were covered with climbers, the borders filled with shrubs and herbaceous perennials, and beds around a central stone water basin spill over with *Alchemilla mollis* and other low-growing plants. Here, too, there is clever use of Dawyck beech, the narrowly fastigiate form of common beech, to make tall columns to accent the design.

There are two little enclosures close to the point at which the tithe barn extends into the garden. One is a small herb garden, simple yet effective, a recent addition made by Lady Ashbrook; the other, known as the Flag garden, a little stone-paved garden made in 1900 by Mrs Piers Egerton-Warburton for roses, herbaceous perennials and lavender. Now, with one of its walls realigned, the beauty of the tithe barn is better displayed.

To the west of the big walled garden there is an entirely new wild garden with many young trees, a little orchard-like in effect, and to the east of the mansion, entirely divorced from the main garden, near a place where Miss Jekyll recorded 'an old parterre of a kind now seldom seen out of Italy; with elaborate scrolls and arabesques of clipped box' there is, in a woodland, a shrub collection made by Viscountess Ashbrook's son.

Alchemilla mollis

Lanhydrock Park

The guide books state quite correctly that Lanhydrock is situated two-and-a-half miles south of Bodmin off the Bodmin to Lostwithiel road, so that is the route along which most visitors approach it. If their objective is mainly to see the famous long gallery in the north wing of the mansion with its delightful plastered ceiling depicting in high relief scenes from the Old Testament, it will matter little, but if it is the park and garden that has attracted them to Lanhydrock a less obvious route will provide a more exciting approach. They should come, not from Bodmin, but from Liskeard following the Lostwithiel road but forking right by the tumuli beyond West Taphouse on to the minor road to Cutmadoc. Within a mile they will be cresting Bofarnel Downs by another group of tumuli and suddenly the whole 200 acre estate of Lanhydrock will come into view spread out on the far western slope of the valley of the River Fowey.

The fine Tudor house, built of local grey granite, will be just visible nestling beneath its sheltering hill but what will really cause the visitor to halt in admiration will be the park itself. It is bisected by a double avenue of trees running straight up the facing slope to the house. This avenue is flanked by areas of grassland, liberally sprinkled with fine specimen trees, the whole framed in well varied woodland. If it is spring or early summer even from this two mile distance the glow of rhododendrons will be visible above the house and all summer through there will be the varied purple and copper shades of beech to contrast with the many greens of other trees.

Dropping down 500 feet in a mile the traveller will cross the river on the outskirts of Cutmadoc, enter the avenue he has already viewed so dramatically from above and begin the gentle ascent to the gatehouse. In a county famed for its beautiful gardens, Lanhydrock remains astonishingly little appreciated. Certainly it does not boast such vast collections of exotic shrubs as some Cornish gardens, but it has been stocked with discrimination over a period of 100 years and it has what so many Cornish gardens lack, a firm and altogether satisfying design. The house itself is beautiful and the garden provides it with a perfect setting.

Lanhydrock has a long history and throughout has remained in the same family. Inheritance has not always been by the male line, so names of owners have changed, but descendants of Richard Roberts, or Robartes, who was created a baron and who bought the house in 1620, have continued to live at Lanhydrock for over 300 years and have developed it with skill and affection. In 1953 it was given by Viscount Clifden to the National Trust. There was one brief interlude, quite early in its history, when the second Lord Robartes, having declared himself for parliament, was driven from Lanhydrock in 1644 by Sir Richard Grenville, who held it for a while. But Lord Robartes was soon back again and by 1648 he was planting the great avenue of sycamores, which remains to this day. It is astonishing that sycamores should have survived so well, but the trees are approaching the end of their life and are now partnered by beeches which will eventually take their place.

Opposite: The terraces and one of the large bronze urns which are a feature of Lanhydrock Park

At this early period, the mansion had four wings built around a central quadrangle so that the avenue could be seen only from the eastern windows. Towards the end of the 18th century the eastern wing was removed completely, so opening up the whole quadrangle to the park.

The mansion itself is a fairly restrained example of the Tudor style. In front of it, however, stands a much more flamboyant two-storey gate-house with two octagonal turrets. It was completed by the second baron in 1651, is lavishly decorated with little ball-topped obelisks, carved panels, arches and columns. At that time it was joined to the house by walls, but now it stands alone – a highly conspicuous and romantic object in the landscape and a key feature in the design of the garden. Not only does it stand at the head of the avenue, making a focal point both for it and the house, but it also marks the division between the park and the formal terraces around the house which it dominates from almost every view-point.

The terraces were a much later addition made in 1857 by Thomas James Agar, who, 12 years later, was created Baron Robartes of Lanhydrock, the previous title having lapsed in 1764. The terraces, which wrap around the house to east and north, are at slightly different levels and are enclosed by a low battlemented stone wall decorated with little obelisks in the same style as those on the gatehouse. Some are further enclosed by low hedges of box, while others are adorned with tall, cone-shaped specimens of Irish yew, arranged in soldierly ranks. Entirely plain parterres of grass are contrasted with others filled with elaborately patterned beds filled with roses and bedding plants in season.

There are also handsome bronze urns. Cherubs sit beside one, heads cupped in hands, gravely contemplating the interior. Another carries masks of Bacchus and vines in high relief. The slender handles of a third are fashioned like fabulous animals. All are said to be the work of Louis Ballin, goldsmith to Louis XIV. They may have been made for the Chateau de Bagatelle, where they certainly were in the middle of the 19th century. Bequest brought them to England, eventually to Nether Swell in Gloucestershire, from where they were purchased by the second Lord Robartes of Lanhydrock, perhaps as part of the reconstruction necessary after a great fire in 1881 had destroyed much of the mansion. This was immediately rebuilt in the original manner under the direction of Mr Richard Coad. The urns were certainly in place by 1903 as they appear in photographs taken then.

The terraces were not the only additions made by Thomas James Agar. He also developed the area to the north of the house, now known as the Higher Garden, and much of what he planned there remains, though the planting must now be very different. For here are many fine shrubs, including species of rhododendron, that would not have been available in 1860 when the garden was first laid out.

Ornamental bronze urns

A curling hedge of yew screens what is now a herbaceous garden and there are good magnolias, Japanese maples, camellias and many other fine trees and shrubs. Here too, backed by bamboos is a Holy Well. The partly sunken building that protects it looks rather like an ice-house and was probably built as a feature for this Higher Garden, though the well itself is ancient. There are other buildings, including a large 15th century tithe barn and what was once a gardener's cottage, picturesquely clothed with climbing plants, including the rather tender *Campsis radicans* with its trumpet-shaped orange flowers. A brick pillared pergola was added much later and provides support for clematis and other climbers.

Viscount Clifden inherited Lanhydrock from his father, the second Baron Robartes of Lanhydrock. Further extension and replanting was carried out in the manner of most 20th-century garden planting in Cornwall, which was to exploit the mild climate and moderately acid soil for the cultivation of a great variety of exotic trees and shrubs. Some of this planting has already been noted in the Higher Garden. Much more is on the hill behind the house and the little church of St Hydroc which nestles beside it. A broad winding path ascends this hill between trees and shrubs planted as individual specimens or in small groups in rough cut grass. From the summit of the hill one can peer down through the great beech trees and over the rhododendrons and coloured maples into the terrace gardens, viewing the Tudor gatehouse from above and beyond it glimpsing the beginning of the great avenue.

The Tudor gatehouse

From this point a little gateway gives entrance to the Great Wood, an old plantation now underplanted with still more rhododendrons, including, on some of the more sheltered slopes to the east, some of the large-leaved Himalayan species always most effective when viewed, as here, from above. By way of the top ride the visitor can return to the drive and gatehouse, or, if he prefers, may continue his journey through the wood for a full half mile to the southern extremity of the estate, returning by way of the avenue.

Ascott

Ascott, between Leighton Buzzard and Wing, in Buckinghamshire, is more famous for its art collection than for its garden. It was mainly for its furniture, pictures and porcelain that it was accepted by the National Trust in 1949 as a gift from the late Anthony de Rothschild, and today these art treasures are as well preserved and skilfully displayed as ever. Yet it is probable that of the many thousands who visit Ascott each year, the majority come primarily to see the gardens. This is not surprising, for Ming and K'ang Hsi porcelain are highly cultivated tastes and even French furniture or old Dutch and English masters, though more readily appreciated, are unlikely to be highly popular attractions.

Gardens need no expertise to make them enjoyable, least of all when they have as many unexpected and interesting features as those of Ascott, and such a delightful setting. Here are all the elements dear to the ordinary garden-lover: well-kept lawns, fine trees, handsome evergreens, well-trimmed topiary specimens, romantic sculpture and gay flowers. But, of

Opposite: The Lily Pond

Right: The view looking down the Dutch Garden at Ascott

*The topiary sundial created
out of clipped yew and box*

course, there is more to a garden than that which instantly meets the eye, and to me Ascott remains an intriguing enigma. For one thing, though it is a Victorian garden containing all the major elements associated with its period, they are assembled in an unusual way, almost, one might say, in reverse. For another, though the garden is still barely a hundred years old and some very famous people were concerned with its creation, remarkably little has been recorded about it and few firm facts are available today.

Those that are known can be briefly stated. Ascott was originally a farmhouse, completed in 1606. In 1875 it was purchased with its farmland by Baron Nathan Meyer de Rothschild, who lived near by at Tring. The following year it was taken over by his brother, Leopold de Rothschild, who lived at Gunnersbury House and wanted Ascott mainly for use as a hunting box. Very soon he was employing the architect George Devey to enlarge the little farmhouse, and this he did so thoroughly that it more or less disappeared within a large, rather rambling building in the black-and-white Tudor style.

At about this time the famous Chelsea nursery, James Veitch and Sons, was entrusted with the task of laying out the garden. Sir Harry Veitch, who had been head of the firm since the death of his father in 1869, took personal control, though who actually determined the style and drew the plans is not clear. But what is certain from early pictures is that by 1900 the garden was complete, with all the main features much as they are today, though there have since been alterations in detail.

One factor which almost certainly influenced both design and planting was that at this period Ascott was used mainly in winter. It remained for many years a hunting box, and this probably explains the extensive use of evergreen trees and shrubs, and in particular of evergreens with variegated foliage. Ascott is in an exposed position, and the evergreens, and also the many fine deciduous trees that were planted with them, must have

116

provided much-needed shelter as well as colour at a season when it would be particularly welcome.

But none of this explains what I have called the reverse arrangement of the major elements in the Ascott design. There are, as one would expect at this period, both formal and natural features, but what is surprising is to find that in general the freer styles are used around the house, and the farther one moves away from it the more one is conscious of man in complete control.

The house is approached from the Leighton Buzzard–Aylesbury road by a curving drive. To the left, as one enters, is the cricket ground. To the right is a large area, known as 'the field'. The latter is planted with specimen trees rather too widely spaced for this to be called an arboretum, but nevertheless containing some fine specimens, including the Algerian oak, *Quercus canariensis*, which in mild winters retains its large, shining green leaves until February.

To the north the house is largely closed in by various outbuildings, cottages, the kitchen garden and greenhouses, though there is a wide grass walk which leads through these to a large oval lake, the lily pool, which has always been one of the admired features of Ascott. Mr de Rothschild, it appears, was very fond of water lilies, though even here one is reminded of the sporting interests which the place was originally designed to serve, the romantic little thatched shed which stands beside the pool still being known as the skating hut. The main garden is to the south of the house where the land flows down into the Vale of Aylesbury. At first one is aware only of smooth turf and trees, the lawn in places terraced with shallow grass banks linking the different levels, in others following more closely the natural contours of the land. The trees are planted as isolated specimens, more closely spaced than those in 'the field' and containing a greater variety of ornamental species, including a good *Acer griseum*, some scarlet oaks and copper beeches. There are two mulberries, maybe left over from the original farmhouse garden, and away to the west quite a large, apparently natural, dell is planted with cherries. It is all very informal in a well-ordered kind of way.

The real surprises are yet to come. Cross the grass terraces and the visitor will discover that virtually the whole southern perimeter of the garden is ringed with formal features of the most intriguing kind. Already one may have noticed a few topiary specimens standing around in somewhat unexpected places, but here they multiply greatly and push out like giant Daleks advancing into the meadows.

To the extreme east is perhaps the oddest of all these formal features, a giant sundial entirely cut in yew and box. The central gnomon is actually composed of two different varieties of yew, golden on top and Irish below. Elsewhere in the garden one may observe balls of golden yew top grafted on to stout bare stems of yew, and here someone seems to have had the bright idea of letting the stock grow as well as the scion to produce the two coloured gnomon, shaped rather like a giant egg in an egg-cup. The Roman figures of the dial are cut in golden box with a motto on the southern side in golden yew. Its message is 'light and shade by turn but love always', and there are hearts cut in golden yew at each end.

117

Below, facing the meadows, is a straight walk backed by a high sunny wall, with a little colonnaded pavilion, the Tea House, at the eastern end. Rather tender things like wintersweet, garrya and various kinds of ceanothus grow against the wall and it is known, of course, as the Madeira Walk.

Continuing westwards along this strange boundary of elaborately formal features, past more large topiary specimens, one arrives at a circular garden, hedged in yew and containing a magnificent fountain group depicting Venus in a shell-chariot, attended by cherubs and drawn by sea-horses. It was made by an American, William Wetmore Story who also made the huge shell fountain at Cliveden.

Continuing west, the scene changes to one of well-groomed informality as one crosses an area where there was once a shallow pool, though the only

The spectacular fountain at Ascott depicting Venus in a shell chariot

remaining evidence of this is a depression in the ground and two fine swamp cypresses. These seem to have suffered no harm from the loss of water over their roots, despite the fact that the pool was drained at least 40 years ago.

From this point one can turn southwards into the older of two commemorative groves, this one planted by Leopold de Rothschild in 1897 for Queen Victoria's Jubilee. There is a specially fine *Parrotia persica* to admire here, fully 33 feet in diameter, also a shapely manna ash, a paper birch and a cut-leaved beech. Like all the tree plantations at Ascott, there are thousands of naturalised daffodils, and here are also fritillaries which were probably introduced but thrive as if native to the site.

Then on again through what was once an apple orchard and has now been converted into an avenue of red-twigged limes, which marks the south-western extremity of the 45-acre garden. Turning north past the remains of the original rock garden and fernery, one arrives at the last and largest of the formal features, the Dutch Garden. This is long and relatively narrow, enclosed by high banks of shrubs and closed in at the far end by a Victorian grotto which can be mounted by stone steps between blocks of tufa, so that from its summit one can look down on the shaped beds, still filled with appropriate changes of bedding plants for spring and summer. This garden is also dominated by a fountain designed by Story, this one tall and elegant, with tiered basins surmounted by a bronze figure of Mercury. One of the outer hedges of the Dutch Garden provides a background for curved herbaceous borders which have just been completely remade after many years of partial neglect.

From these it is only a short step to the rustic simplicity of the dell and the more self-conscious casualness of the tree collection in front of the house. It is said that Leopold de Rothschild desired a garden 'in no one style', a not unusual aspiration in what was one of Britain's most experimental periods in garden making. What makes Ascott unique is the way in which those contrasted styles are associated.

Hever Castle

Few privately owned gardens consistently draw such large numbers of visitors as Hever Castle whenever they are open to the public. It is not difficult to see why, for Hever combines romance and beauty with an element of eccentricity which is highly intriguing, plus a fine and extensive plant collection. The castle near Edenbridge in Kent is tiny, really no more than a moated manor house despite its turrets and drawbridge.

Anne Boleyn was born and brought up at Hever and there is still a quiet path through the meadows on higher ground to the south which is known as Anne Boleyn's Walk and which may well have been used by her. But the low-lying land was marshy, and there was probably little or no garden around Hever Castle at that time. What the visitor enjoys today has been entirely created since 1903 when the property was purchased by William Waldorf Astor, who had been American Minister in Rome and who later adopted British nationality and was created 1st Viscount Astor of Hever.

Mr Astor, as he then was, set about the improvement of his property with energy and originality. Since the castle was too small to contain his servants and guests, he created a little village in Tudor style behind it to provide the necessary accommodation without in any way interfering with the historic building.

For the garden itself his plans were even bolder and more unusual. While in Rome he had amassed a considerable collection of statues, sculptures and objects of antiquarian interest and he wanted a place in in the Italian manner expressly for this purpose. Since this would be out of character with the little Tudor castle, he placed it some distance away,

1st Viscount Astor of Hever

separated by lawns and an outer moat which helped to drain the wet land.

From traditional English landscape gardening he borrowed the idea of creating a large artificial lake in the middle distance (this too, was useful for drainage), but this he partly concealed from the house by the Italian garden which abuts it. Even so, the lake is not immediately revealed even when one enters the Italian garden, for it is hidden by a massive stone loggia which straddles the farther end of the garden. Only as one comes around this on to the colonnaded terrace which overlooks the lake does the full grandeur of the scheme confront one. The terrace itself is dominated by an immense marble fountain bowl, flanked by female figures, which was specially commissioned for the purpose.

Because of the complexity of its design the garden is full of further surprises. Tucked away between the cloister-like pergola and the high wall which separates it from the rose garden is a long grotto, known as the Gallery of Fountains, dripping with water and filled with ferns and other moisture loving plants. J. Cheal and Sons carried out much of the constructional work at Hever and Mr Joseph Cheal was sent to Italy to study Renaissance gardens there and particularly the gardens of the Villa d'Este at Tivoli which had greatly delighted Lord Astor.

The rose garden itself follows the conventional Edwardian style with numerous geometric beds for bedding roses planted in blocks of a kind.

The sundial garden at Hever Castle

However it is made distinctive by some of Lord Astor's antiquities which decorate it so freely. The main collection, including statues, busts, columns, sarcophagi, huge Ali-Baba urns and other objects, is disposed in the Italian garden, mainly in the long border and against the stone wall on its northern side where the exhibits peer out from a bower of plants.

Tucked into the angle between the Italian and the rose garden is a rock garden constructed with massive blocks of native sandstone. Ascending this by rocky steps the visitor will discover a long herbaceous border planted mainly in shades of blue and yellow and previously concealed by hedges and banks of rhododendrons, azaleas and other flowering shrubs.

Retracing his steps towards the castle beside this border, he will come upon a little sunken pool ringed with irises and other moisture-loving plants. Beyond this a cascade and stone steps lead up to Anne Boleyn's Walk and an overlook from which some of the best general views of the castle and garden can be obtained.

Those who do not find a two-mile walk too arduous can turn back again at this point and continue their exploration along Anne Boleyn's Walk to a waterfall at the far end of the lake, cross its twin feed-ways by footbridges and return to the castle down the magnificent chestnut avenue.

Between the inner and outer moats on the west side of the castle is a little meadow filled with daffodils in spring and on the east side a series of secret gardens, including a small but complex maze, a sundial garden and a little enclosure dominated by a set of immense topiary chessmen formed from golden yew. These chessmen were specially formed for Hever in the Cheal nursery at Crawley to designs made by Lord Astor himself from illustrations he had found in the British Museum depicting chessmen in use during the reign of Henry VIII. Despite the close involvement of professionals such as the Cheals and also the architect F.L. Pearson, who designed the Tudor village and was almost certainly consulted about the garden, it does appear that it was Lord Astor who was the master planner.

The one formal feature of this remarkable garden that does stand fully revealed from the outset is the elegant half-moon pool placed outside the Italian garden where it faces the castle. This simple semi-circular pool is framed in stone, backed by dark green yew, flanked by large beds of currant-red 'Rosemary Rose', and dominated by a white marble statue of Venus. It is a fitting introduction to a garden which succeeds in uniting in a remarkable manner ideas from many different garden-making traditions with some which are peculiarly its own.

Opposite: The rose garden

Right: Some of the statuary in the Italian garden

Mount Stewart

The gardens of Mount Stewart in Co. Down are now among the loveliest to be found anywhere in the British Isles, yet at the time of the First World War Lady Londonderry could describe this as the dampest, darkest and saddest place she had ever stayed in. It cannot always have been so, for the house is a noble building, well-proportioned and magnificently situated beside the eastern shore of Strangford Lough between Newtonards and Grey Abbey. It appears to have started in the latter half of the 18th century as a medium-sized house and to have been considerably enlarged a generation later. The south-western front is especially beautiful; long and low with a good pediment above a colonnaded porchway all of the same grey stone.

To the east and south-east the land rises, though not to any great height, for the Irish Sea is only four miles away across the narrow peninsula which here curls southwards from Belfast Lough. The garden was probably landscaped when the first house was built. Certainly nearly a mile to the south, on a little hill overlooking the lough, stands an elegant two-storey octagonal stone pavilion, in the manner of the Temple of the Winds at Shugborough Park in Staffordshire, which is known to have been built about 1765, and, like it, very probably to the design of James (Athenian) Stuart.

The Italian Garden at Mount Stewart

One of the monkey pillars which line one side of the Italian Garden

Many of the fine old trees that still grow at Mount Stewart must have been planted at about this period and maybe it was then that the six acre lake was made beneath the hill to the east of the house, for it is precisely the kind of mid-distance feature beloved of late 18th-century landscape gardeners.

At its prime this must have been a very attractive garden with 'nature' reigning supreme and man's handiwork safely concealed in a walled kitchen garden a mile away. Yet by the time the 7th Marquess of Londonderry inherited Mount Stewart in 1915 nature had gained too great an ascendency, trees pressed in upon the house from every side, and the woods were choked with *Rhododendron ponticum*.

Lady Londonderry determined to effect a complete transformation in this dreary scene, and in this she was greatly assisted by two circumstances. Immediately after the war she had an ample labour force, for this was a period of depression in Northern Ireland when landowners had been asked to assist by undertaking whatever improvements might seem desirable. She also had the enthusiastic support and advice of two eminent plant lovers, Sir John Ross of Bladensburg and Sir Herbert Maxwell of Monreith, both of whom inspired in her a wish to grow many of the exotic trees and shrubs for which the mild climate of Mount Stewart seemed specially favourable.

The gardens she planned and made with so much success were mainly formal in design, in large measure inspired by what she had seen in travels in Italy, Spain and Portugal, yet so rich and varied was the planting, so swift and luxuriant the subsequent growth, that masonry quickly became clothed with vegetation and the final product was anything but formal in effect. Once, all the visitors approached the simpler eastern front of the house by a curling drive. The drive is still there, its flanks greatly enriched by new planting, but now that the gardens belong to the National Trust, garden visitors enter more secretly by a gate beside the lough at the south-western corner of the garden. This approach is far less impressive but it has its merits in that the visitor emerges from a narrow and rather dark pathway and through a little grove of dracaenas (*Cordyline indivisa*) directly into the magnificent Italian garden and one of the finest views of the lovely south-west facade.

The scene is rich beyond description. In front of the house, extending from bow to bow is a wide flagged terrace, balustraded to match the house, with stone steps leading down to the garden 10 feet below. This is a large rectangle divided by a wide central grass walk into two identical parterres, the design of each copied from the south-western parterre at Dunrobin Castle, the home of Lady Londonderry's mother. Originally this was planned as a display garden with bedding plants in season, but when mounting costs and labour shortage made it impossible to continue with this the design was simplified and the planting was made semi-permanent. Herbaceous perennials rub shoulders with flowering shrubs, roses with annuals and bedding plants, the whole reminiscent of cottage garden planting, but more controlled and on a vastly grander scale. There is symmetry in the plan but little in the planting. Even the circular pools which centre each parterre are planted differently, one ringed with crimson astilbes, the other with hostas, ferns and lilac-pink water irises. The beds, too, are not all outlined with box, but have various edgings, some of dwarf hebes, others of lavender, rue, heather and other small shrubby plants. The flame flower, *Tropaeolum speciosum*, adds its own blend of tender green and scarlet, for it has been permitted to ramble freely through some of the edgings.

On the south-west side of the Italian Garden wide curving steps lead down to a Spanish garden with an oval pool as a central feature. Tall slender arches formed of clipped *Cupressus macrocarpa* surround it on three sides and the feeling of enclosure is accentuated by a little summer house and flanking walls all topped with green Spanish tiles. This building is set right across a wide avenue cut through the woodland to Strangford Lough, completely concealing it both from this pool garden and from the higher Italian Garden. Only when one mounts to the house terrace does it come into view, revealing that it is lined with date palms and *Rhododendron arboreum* and that it channels a splendid vista to the lough and distant Mourne Mountains. This is a superb conception worthy of a great landscape architect, but in fact Lady Londonderry employed no professional assistance, drew all the plans herself and executed the work with her own home-based labour.

This even applied to the amusing ornaments with which the Italian Garden and the flanking Dodo Terrace are decorated, all of which were made by Thomas Beattie, a local craftsman, to Lady Londonderry's designs. The south-western edge of the Italian Garden is lined with slender stone pillars each bearing a different grinning or scowling mask and surmounted by a monkey bearing a large stone vase. Stone seats link column to column, and the entrance to the Spanish Garden is flanked by taller twin columns surmounted by griffons and plinths with curly-tailed lions.

Even stranger objects appear on the Dodo Terrace besides the four dodos which perch on pillars flanking the stairway leading up to it from the Italian Garden and down from it on the far side into the Mairi Garden planned like a Tudor rose. On the terrace there are rabbits, a dinosaur, frogs, a hedgehog and other animals each representing a member of the Ark Club which was started by Lady Londonderry early in the first World War and met at Londonderry House every Wednesday during the war. Originally intended for the entertainment of the King's messengers when they came back on leave, it soon grew into a considerable gathering of politicians, artists, poets, authors, sailors, soldiers, airmen and others who were her friends. All were called by names of animals, birds or fishes with the same initials as their names and here some are commemorated on Dodo Terrace. Noah's Ark, also in stone, stands centrally between the dodos.

All around there is a profusion of subtropical vegetation. Eucalyptus trees have grown to great size and cordylines tower above the parterres and in places form groves. Huge spiky rosettes of beschorneria grow on the house terrace and extend their slender pink flower stems towards the sun like the necks of craning flamingoes. The house walls are clothed with rare climbers, including the yellow and white Banksian roses and 'Dundee

Opposite: Mature cordylines rise above the permanent planting in the parterres. The Dodo Terrace can be seen in the background

The white stag of the woodland garden

Topiary Irish harp

Opposite: Garden house with roses at Tyninghame

Overleaf: The pergola at Hestercombe

Rambler', and in the Spanish Garden *Lapageria rosea* scrambles happily over one of the hedges. Shrubs that are normally considered difficult and rare are used in this remarkable garden as hedges; *Desfontainea spinosa*, for example, with its holly-like leaves and vermilion flowers, and *Drimys aromatica* with narrow evergreen leaves and ivory flowers. But for a fuller list of the huge collection of plants at Mount Stewart the reader is referred to the excellent guide published by the National Trust.

Away to the north west, by way of a little woodland richly planted with lilies and tree ferns, are more strange shapes carved not in stone but out of living *Cupressus macrocarpa*. A paved garden in the form of a shamrock leaf is completely enclosed by a tall hedge of this cypress surmounted by figures engaged in a hunt. They arrive by coracle, wound a stag with an arrow shot from the bow of an Amazon, but arrive home with nothing better than a hare, the devil having rescued the stag. The idea was taken from Mary Tudor's psalter, but like so many borrowed ideas at Mount Stewart, has been ingeniously adapted, for these are no medieval figures but the Stewart family themselves amusingly caricatured. Within the Shamrock Garden are more unusual shapes, including a large bear and an Irish harp both formed of yew.

All these elaborate specimens were grown through wire frames made by a smith in the Clogher Valley, Co Tyrone, to Lady Londonderry's designs. There are also some good stone vases and plant troughs in this garden and the Red Hand of Ulster, the hand which McDonnell cut off and threw ashore in the race of the Scottish chieftains to claim the land as their own. The hand is cut out of the paving and was once planted with scarlet tulips. Later this was changed to *Iresine herbstii*, but now, to save labour, it is of dwarf red heather.

From this topiary garden one can walk straight into a garden on the north-west side of the house. This is rectangular in shape, surrounded by a massive stone pillared pergola and largely planted in shades of blue, yellow and flame. At one period the vivid orange-red *Azalea coccinea speciosa* virtually rings the garden, displayed against ceanothus and wisteria. Later there are blue geraniums, campanulas and many roses.

The old woodlands, too, have been thinned, cleared and replanted with a great variety of good shrubs. Rhododendrons of many kinds, including the large-leaved species, thrive in this mild and moist climate. There are good magnolias, including the early flowering *M. campbellii*, davidias and many more, with lilies happily naturalised among them.

After the ornamental curiosities of the formal gardens it is no surprise to emerge into an open glade as one ascends the hill to find a white, life-size stag standing there, silhouetted against the trees, but this is not the last unusual feature of the Mount Stewart gardens. Right at the summit of the hill, overlooking the woodland, the lake, the house and the lough is another formal garden, a burial place for the family, known as Tir-N'an Oge, the Land of Eternal Youth. It is elaborately paved and beautiful terracotta jars stand in niches on the low wall which surround it. A stone-built pavilion towers high above it commanding the finest views of all and statues of St Patrick and St Bridget stand guard on each side of the elaborate wrought iron gate which leads into this very private garden.

The Outdoor Decorators

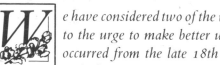

e have considered two of the ways in which British gardeners responded to the urge to make better use of the vast influx of exotic plants that occurred from the late 18th century onwards. Some made collections and often to a very considerable extent allowed the plants to dictate the design, and others went in for spectacular display, using glasshouses to enable them to prepare successive batches of plants which could be moved into the gardens as they approached the peak of their beauty.

Though both methods were capable of producing gardens of considerable interest and beauty, neither satisfied a number of garden makers who were repelled by the lack of cohesion of the collections and the propensity for vulgarity of the display. They sought methods of garden making that were highly organised and yet subtle, that delighted all the senses and extracted the maximum of beauty from all the plants which were used. Design was the operative word, and though these garden makers are often referred to as picture makers their art had, and still has, for it continues undiminished to the present day, a great deal more in common with that of interior decorators than with painters. What they were seeking to create were not three dimensional pictures, nor even a whole evolving series of such pictures to be looked at from particular viewpoints or to be unfolded in a carefully considered sequence, but complete environments in which to live and move. This is an almost exact parallel with the aims of skilful house decorators and furnishers who consider each room as a place in which people are going to live and perform certain functions. They must, therefore, provide the right setting and induce the appropriate mood, gay, restful, amusing or even plain utilitarian.

It is impossible to say when this particular style of gardening started, for to some degree it has existed from the very beginning. Even when formal gardens were at their most grand or landscape gardens were reaching out to the horizon, garden owners were creating for themselves more intimate areas in which they could find peace and seclusion, and maybe a greater expression of their own personalities. However by the mid-19th century this was a movement that was gaining momentum and at the close of the century it acquired an articulate advocate who was to give it a direction and sense of purpose which it had previously somewhat lacked.

This was a middle-aged lady named Gertrude Jekyll, a comfortably-off spinster who had spent the whole of her life in the company of cultivated people. She knew William Morris and John Ruskin well and shared many of their ideas. She was an amateur painter with considerable talent, and she had a special admiration for the work of Turner which she spent much time in copying. She enjoyed music, played the piano and was skilful in a number of crafts including carving, carpentry, embroidery and photography. She was also so good at interior decoration that her assistance was sought by many of her friends, among them the Duke of Westminster who in 1875 was completing alterations and extensions at Eaton Hall which necessitated a great deal of refurnishing and decorating.

Miss Jekyll was already short sighted and her eyesight continued to deteriorate until in 1891 she was advised by a specialist to cut down drastically on all work, such as embroidery and painting, that might strain her eyes. Two years before she had become friendly with a young architect, Edwin (later to become Sir Edwin) Lutyens. These two events changed the whole course of her life and gave a new impetus to that element in garden making which I have called 'outdoor decorating'.

Lutyens was as impressed by traditional styles and craftsmanship as was Miss Jekyll. He liked to design the gardens for his houses, but was delighted to leave it to Miss Jekyll to suggest the planting for they saw eye to eye on such matters. For her part she loved the Lutyens style, employed him to design her own house Munstead Wood, and clothed his often elaborate stonework with a rich tapestry of plants in which colour and texture were always interwoven with great skill. As the years went by she worked for many other architects and private clients, and by the time of her death in 1932 she had had something to say about more than 300 gardens in Britain, and by her writings in magazines and books had influenced an untold number of others.

That influence continues today, though more usually at second or third hand than direct from her writings or the gardens she herself made. The books are out of print and only to be obtained from libraries. Many of the gardens have disappeared or been so greatly altered that they convey no idea of Miss Jekyll's genius. But a few remain and others, which either derived from her or were inspired by similar ideals, live on and are among the best loved gardens in Britain today. It is an odd fact that when foreign visitors speak with admiration of 'the English garden' it is rarely the great achievements of the 18th-century landscape architects that they have in mind, but the far more cozy garden making which could be called 'the Jekyll style'.

Hestercombe

An inevitable hazard with gardens that rely heavily on herbaceous plants, as nearly all the gardens of the decorators did, is that they require constant intelligent management with frequent replanting if they are to retain their character and quality. It is the nature of herbaceous plants, whether perennial, monocarpic or annual, to grow rapidly and make their full effect in a short time. The annuals must be replaced every year and annual replacements for the monocarpic kinds must also be raised from seed if a continuous sequence is to be maintained. Even the perennials require care to prevent them from growing out of scale or losing vigour for lack of division and replanting.

For all these reasons gardens in which herbaceous plants predominate are highly vulnerable to changes in ownership or even to changing interests on the part of the same owner. Few survive in anything like their original state for more than a generation or so, and this has been the fate of a great many gardens that Miss Jekyll designed either whole or in part. Where she collaborated with an architect the bones of the design probably remain but with planting so different in sensitivity and imagination from that which Miss Jekyll planned that they no longer give any idea of her style. However a few do remain much as she intended, the iris garden at Barrington Court near Ilminster among them, and one of her most renowned collaborations with Lutyens, at Hestercombe also in Somerset near Taunton, has been painstakingly restored.

Hestercombe is not a Lutyens house but he was engaged in 1904 by the then owner, Viscount Portman, to design an entirely new garden and he handed over the entire planting of this to Gertrude Jekyll. After Viscount Portman's death in 1942 the garden was progressively neglected and would almost certainly have disappeared had it not been for a succession of happy chances.

Hestercombe passed into the ownership of the Crown Commissioners who leased it in 1953 to the Somerset County Council for use as head-quarters for the County Fire Service. One gardener was employed to keep the garden in some kind of shape but already much of its distinctive plant-ing had disappeared and it is unlikely that anyone in the Fire Service had even heard of Miss Jekyll. However, from time to time interested visitors arrived to enquire about the garden and it gradually dawned on the tenants that they were occupying a property of some historical and aesthetic interest. The Crown Estate Commissioners were consulted and eventually the County Council undertook to repair the Lutyens architec-ture, some of which was in very bad condition, and to replant the garden.

A great deal of research was carried out to find out exactly what plants Miss Jekyll had recommended when the garden was originally laid out and though it was not possible to obtain all these, since some of the varieties had disappeared from cultivation, the most similar available varieties were used. So Hestercombe lives again as a reasonably authentic example of the work of Lutyens and Jekyll.

It is from every point of view a remarkable garden which will come as a surprise to those who think mainly of Miss Jekyll as a 'natural' planter concerned with woodland and wild gardens or the pretty cottage gardens of the Surrey villages. At Hestercombe the design is uncompromisingly formal and rather ostentatious. The house stands on the extreme southerly slopes of the Quantock Hills with extensive views over Taunton itself to

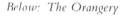
Below: The Orangery

the distant Blackdown Hills. The land has been terraced in such a way as to exaggerate the really quite gentle slope. The top terrace juts out above the garden like the poop of a ship providing a panoramic view of garden and countryside. Below it is a large rectangle, the central portion of which is square and at a lower level than the long strips or walkways which enclose it on three sides. This area, known as The Platt, is divided by wide grass paths laid in the form of a St Andrew's cross. Flights of curved steps lead down into it at each corner. The raised strips on each side carry narrow rills each with three small pools or 'tanks' breaking the otherwise completely straight lines. At their southern end the rills run into little

The Platt at Hestercombe

circular pools. A substantially constructed pergola with stone pillars alternately square and circular in section and heavy timber rafters, runs the length of the raised strip. A 'grey walk' beneath the house terrace completes the rectangle. On descending to this intermediate level it becomes apparent that there are still more architectural features to be admired.

Cavern-like niches are formed in the high terrace wall, centred on the rills and containing circular water basins which repeat the curves of the domes. Each niche is surmounted by a wall fountain which spouts a simple jet which also falls in a curve matching those of the niches and their basins. It is all very clever and extremely effective.

There is more of similar character to the east of the top terrace. Leaving this by way of a circular court known as the Rotunda with a circular pool filled to its rim with still water, one descends another flight of stone steps to reach a long terrace on which stands a handsome orangery apparently straight out of the 17th century though in fact it is all part of the Lutyens' design. In front of it is a large lawn with some old trees and beyond it stone steps lead up to a little rectangular paved garden with formal flower beds. It is known as the Dutch Garden. To the west of the top terrace, balancing the area occupied by the Rotunda, there is a small formal rose garden and arbours.

This rather bare account gives no idea of the elaborate and constantly changing stonework, always a major feature in any Lutyens garden. Nor can it convey any notion of the planting with which Miss Jekyll put beautiful flesh on to the already shapely architectural skeleton. This is at its most luxuriant in the Grey Walk (in fact there is a lot of blue and purple and some pink as well as grey and silver) beneath the top terrace and also over the pergola which forms the southern boundary of the garden. Plants that are massed in the Grey Walk include lavenders, nepeta, rosemary, ceratostigma, echinops, eryngium, *Achillea* 'The Pearl', *Olearia scilloniensis*, phlomis, santolina, *Stachys lanata*, cerastium, *Cineraria maritima* and several kinds of yucca for which Miss Jekyll had an especial affection.

The pergola is covered in vines, clematis, honeysuckles, jasmines, passion flowers and other plants that make it a real covered walk and the Rill Terraces are also richly planted, with more variety in colour including African marigolds, oriental poppies, scarlet bergamot, verbascums, red hot pokers, flag irises, Michaelmas daisies and alstroemerias.

Niche sheltering a circular pool covered with water lilies

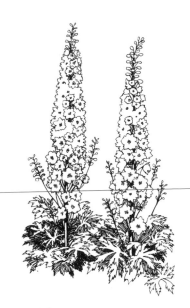

Delphinium

The large, more or less triangular, beds in the Platt are not filled with gaudy bedding-out plants but are semi-permanently planted with bergenias, aconites, Belladonna delphiniums, white peonies and pink China roses. Though some of these are quite large plants they are carefully placed to avoid any blurring of the pattern of this area which is essentially a parterre in the 17th-century manner and, like all good parterres, can be viewed from above.

In fact Hestercombe might be described as a 17th-century formal garden that does not deal in mystery or seek to lure the visitor on by tantalising peeps of features not immediately revealed. On the contrary it displays itself proudly so that in a few moments the visitor has acquired a complete understanding of the design, leaving only the details of construction and planting to be slowly discovered and savoured. The late Christopher Hussey once described it as the greatest Lutyens-Jekyll collaboration. Personally I would not rate it quite as high but it is undoubtedly a very impressive garden which had a great influence on other gardens of the period. It also has the great merit that, thanks to faithful restoration, it can be seen today very much as Lutyens and Jekyll created it.

Hidcote Manor

The garden of Hidcote Manor expresses the ideas of the outdoor decorators as fully and revealingly as any I know in Britain. If one is to regard garden designing in much the same way as interior decorating, with plants taking the place of paintwork and furnishings, how much more fun to have a number of separate rooms each with its own distinctive design and colour scheme. This is exactly what Major Lawrence Johnston produced on what had previously been a completely open and very exposed site on the top of the Cotswold Hills, only a few miles from Chipping Campden.

Hidcote Manor is a pleasant dwelling house built of Cotswold stone in the traditional style of the district. It was already old when Major Johnston purchased it in 1905, but it had never acquired a garden of any note and whatever was there at the time he arrived soon disappeared under the elaborate reconstruction on which he embarked.

As gardens of that period go it is not large, approximately 10 acres in all, but because of the way it is broken up into numerous separate units, each completely self-contained and yet all intimately associated, it seems very much bigger. Somewhat surprisingly, though the garden embraces the house on three sides it does not really provide a setting for the house and from most parts of the garden it is either invisible or nearly so. This is not a garden to be looked at constantly through windows, but one to be visited, walked in, enjoyed and then left for a while. It is the same principle as that which Henry Hoare applied so successfully at Stourhead, but the gardens that resulted could scarcely be more different. Stourhead is a pictorial garden with open views planned on the largest scale. Hidcote is a series of intimate enclosures, few of them of much size and several quite tiny. It is an inward looking garden and one must pass out of it through the wrought iron gates at the head of the main axis to appreciate the fact that it could have made use of superb views across the Vale of Evesham to the distant Malvern Hills.

The two largest enclosures are also the simplest in planting. One is planned as an open-air theatre and encompasses some large beeches, possibly 200 years old. Apart from these and a few specimen trees at the entrance it is simply covered in close mown grass and enclosed by a high hedge of neatly trimmed yew.

Set at right angles to this and centred on it so that in plan it makes a large T, is a narrow avenue, the Long Walk, also grassed and enclosed by high hedges of hornbeam. It is terminated by wrought iron gates used purely as an ornament since it leads into a field of no special interest or beauty.

On paper this basic design looks impressive but on the ground it is difficult to remain aware of it since the two areas are completely screened from one another and it is impossible to pass directly from one into the other. By the time one has turned around corners and passed through several heavily planted areas it is difficult to recollect just how the two are linked in plan. It is perhaps, a reminder of the fact that Major Johnston had been trained as an architect and probably enjoyed drawing this logical scheme as a basis for the more intricate features which he proceeded to fill in around it.

Parallel with the theatre he made what is really the main axis of the garden as seen from ground level. It is a long path centred at one end on a large Cedar of Lebanon which, like the beeches, was there when Major

Right: Part of the Red Border at Hidcote with one of the pavilions and the Stilt Garden in the background

Opposite: Mrs Winthrop's Garden

Johnston arrived and must have formed part of an earlier and simpler garden. The path runs through several small gardens in which the colour schemes change, one being mainly planted in shades of blue, mauve, pink and white; another, a small circle, with some yellow; a third consisting of twin borders, planted in reds, purples and coppery orange in summer but with other colours, including the gold of daffodils, in the spring; and a fourth section all green since it is entirely filled with hornbeams grown as standards and then clipped to form strongly rectangular 'boxes' of foliage at about head level. It is appropriately known as the Stilt Garden and at its far end is the second set of wrought iron gates leading to the hillside and the view.

Though these gardens are only revealed as one moves through them the path is open throughout its length so that one can look all the way from the gate to the cedar or vice versa. The ground rises a little towards the gate and advantage has been taken of this to make a sharp change in level where the Red Border abuts the Stilt Garden. A few steps lead upwards here and are flanked by two elegant little pavilions, part Dutch, part Japanese in style. That on the right as one ascends is placed against the high hedge of the Theatre Garden, that on the left is centred on the Long Walk and provides one of the loveliest framed views of it.

The other enclosures are skilfully interwoven around this main axis and the Long Walk. They vary greatly in size, style and planting. Some are in the manner of early Dutch gardens with formal beds and amusing topiary specimens in the shape of doves, columns, cones and such like. Others are essays in the 'natural' style, one a streamside garden full of moisture-loving perennials and another a wild garden in which hardy ferns grow with hardy perennials, shrubs and trees, many of them chosen for their fine autumn colour. This is known as Westonbirt but it really has little in common with that famous Gloucestershire arboretum since not only is it tiny by comparison but has been planted with much greater awareness of design and pictorial effect.

One of the many clever touches is a tiny enclosure known as Mrs Winthrop's Garden. after Major Johnston's mother, planted almost entirely with yellow-flowered or bronze-leaved plants with a circular area paved with russet-purple bricks. It is a little gem of formal design coupled with informal planting and it is placed where it commands a view across Westonbirt which contrasts so strongly in style.

Yet another enclosure is filled with rectangular beds enclosed in clipped box and planted with a medley of herbaceous plants and roses in the cottage manner. Columns of clipped yew are set across it in two straight lines and the hedges of the Stilt Garden provide it with a solid background though, like so much at Hidcote, this is something of an optical illusion since yet another feature is tucked in between the Column Garden and the Stilt Garden. It is known as the Terrace Garden, is long and narrow and is mainly remarkable for a raised bed with some good rock plants and shrubs.

It was typical of Major Johnston's care for detail that his swimming pool was made to fit perfectly into this scheme of open-air rooms. It is a large circular basin contained within mellow sandstone walls and almost completely filling a rectangular enclosed by yew hedges. Magnolias grow around and are reflected in the still water. To one side is a changing room almost completely concealed by hedges and as a background there is an enormous portico of clipped yew leading into a small unplanted circle surrounded by more yew and carpeted with grass.

Elsewhere will be found a rock bank and a little woodland carpeted with periwinkles and other shade-loving plants. To the north of the house there is a water-lily pool, a collection of old roses and mixed-flower borders, but these are more recent additions made since the National Trust took over Hidcote after Major Johnston's death. In his day this was a kitchen garden and nursery, the working area in which plants were prepared and tested before being committed to the ornamental gardens to the south and west.

Sissinghurst Castle

In many respects the garden of Sissinghurst Castle, Kent repeats the lessons of Hidcote Manor, but with an even greater emphasis on the use of plant colour and texture to create harmonious and beautiful effects. Like Hidcote it owes its preservation to the fact that, almost immediately after the death of Sir Harold Nicholson, it was taken over by the National Trust and has therefore been intelligently maintained precisely as its creators would have wished.

Aerial view of Sissinghurst Castle

The first sight of the castle, its twin turrets standing pencil slim above the long, low gatehouse flanked by oast-houses, is always exciting. It is almost impossible to believe that this is a genuine building to be lived and worked in, and not, as would seem more likely, an incredibly realistic film set for some romantic story about the Middle Ages, or, as the late Vita Sackville-West described it when she first saw it in 1930, Sleeping Beauty's Castle, a place which instantly captured her heart and fired her imagination. But at that time the place was in semi-ruin, having been neglected for two centuries and used during that period as a prison, a workhouse and a farm. There were no beautiful gardens such as greet the visitor today, but instead a sea of mud, in which old bedsteads, plough blades and other rubbish were embedded. Yet once this had been a splendid Tudor mansion where Queen Elizabeth I had slept three nights during a Royal Progress through Kent. The tower with its flanking octagonal turrets had been completed only a short while before her arrival and beyond it at that time was the main mansion built around a large quadrangle.

Most of this was pulled down early in the 19th century apart from one fragment retained as a two-storey cottage, and another, a little house built for a priest: they remain today. So, what Vita Sackville-West and her husband, Sir Harold Nicholson, acquired when they purchased the remnants of Sissinghurst Castle was not one house but three, plus a number of farm buildings, and several cottages built in Victorian times. Some they removed and some they restored with great skill and understanding, but the greatest triumph of all was the garden which they jointly planned and planted as a setting for Sleeping Beauty's Castle.

Opposite: The Cottage Garden

Right: The White Garden

Vita Sackville-West

It is a garden which makes use of one of the oldest ideas in garden planning; that is, to split up the available area into a number of more or less rectangular sections, rather like rooms in a house, and give each its own individual decor. This was the kind of design fashionable when Sissinghurst Castle was built and so the original garden might well have been laid out in a similar manner, though no one knows for certain as neither plans nor pictures survive from that time.

But where the new garden differs completely from anything that could conceivably have existed in the 16th century is in the richness and variety of its planting. Old gardens were formal both in overall design and in detail. The ideal which Miss Sackville-West and her husband set themselves was, in her own words, that 'there should be the strictest formality in design, the maximum informality in planting.' It is a recipe that suits the situation perfectly: the geometrical pattern reminds one of the stately past, while the luxuriant planting mirrors the romantic aura of the buildings today.

Because it is a garden divided into numerous compartments there is a sense of intimacy about the place which is very reassuring. One is never overawed by the scale and there are always plenty of useful ideas to be picked up and used at home, even if one has no more than a tiny plot. It is perhaps for this reason that two of the most popular features are the White Garden and the Cottage Garden. Both are quite small and seem complete in themselves. The paths in the White Garden are of brick and the beds are neatly edged with box. There are great drifts of white violets and violas, plumy cream smilacina, billowing clouds of snowy gypsophila, and silver-leaved Scotch thistles standing stiffly erect to partner the nearly-as-tall white delphiniums. In summer the Regal lilies and tumbling sprays of *Rosa filipes* fill the air with their perfume. The only colour is the muted yellow of *Nicotiana* 'Lime Green'.

The Nuttery at Sissinghurst

By contrast the Cottage Garden is full of warm colour; golden globe flowers (trollius), red violas, chestnut broom, smokey crimson irises, sharp yellow Welsh poppies (*Meconopsis cambrica*), copper-coloured sun roses (*helianthemum*), red and yellow aquilegias and then, later in the summer, the tall spires of verbascum; all seen against a backdrop of white, yellow and coppery-pink roses covering the cottage walls. In the centre of it all stands an old burnished copper filled with the red form of *Mimulus glutinosus*. It is a heart-warming sight and one that always sets the cameras clicking as does the rose garden in June and July. This is filled, not with conventional hard-pruned bedding roses, but with old-fashioned and shrub roses permitted to grow into large bushes. Some are so big that they require the support of rustic tripods and they include colours and rich spicy perfumes which are scarcely to be found in modern varieties.

Nor are the roses planted alone, as is the fashion today, but are associated with many other plants, mainly herbaceous perennials and bulbs. Some of the finest irises in the garden are to be found here, as well as sea hollies (eryngium) and ornamental onions (allium) very skilfully blended for colour and leaf character.

Another feature is a pleached-lime avenue with flanking borders filled exclusively with spring flowers. Most of them are low growing plants one would normally associate with rock gardens and are grouped in a very natural manner providing a striking contrast to the meticulous training of the limes.

This avenue leads to a little plantation of nut bushes left over from earlier times. These have been thinned and pruned and were for many years thickly under-planted with polyanthus, the kind of planting that only Vita Sackville-West would have thought of. Unhappily the soil became sick of them and they have had to be replaced with other plants. Beyond this again, at the south-eastern corner of the garden, is another typically Sackville-West creation, a cunningly designed herb garden.

Part of the old moat, which actually pre-dates Sissinghurst Castle itself, forms the eastern and northern boundaries of the garden and encloses an orchard golden with daffodils in spring. The old apple trees there are no longer expected to pay their way, but are retained as ornamental trees and as supports for climbing roses which drip out of them in summer.

It is possible to ascend the tower, and from its summit there is not only a remarkable bird's-eye view of the garden, but also an extensive prospect of the Kentish countryside, to as far as the North Downs, 10 miles distant.

Nymans

Nymans at Handcross, Sussex has enjoyed the twin benefits of passing into the care of the National Trust while still in peak conditions and continuing, even after that, to be cared for by a talented member of the family which created it, the Countess of Rosse, granddaughter of Ludwig Messel. In consequence visitors can feel sure that here they are seeing very much what was intended, not necessarily from the moment garden

Above: The house and mixed border at Nymans

Opposite: The twin herbaceous borders leading to the fountain surrounded by four topiary sculptures

making commenced at Nymans in 1885, for this is a garden that has evolved rather than one that was visualised as an entity from the outset, but certainly as it had matured at the time it was bequeathed to the National Trust by Col L.C.R. Messel in 1954.

Nymans is not a pure example of the Jekyll style, yet it contains sufficient elements of it to justify inclusion in this section. But both Col Messell and his father Ludwig Messel were keen collectors and two of their gardeners, James Comber and his son Harold Comber, shared their delight in new and rare plants. The Messels subscribed to various expeditions in search of new plants and Harold Comber did some valuable collecting of his own in South America.

In consequence it was constantly necessary to extend the garden to make room for new things and eventually it burst right out of its natural boundaries into woodland on the other side of a public road. What developed there was a collector's garden and so one that is outside my present story.

But besides being collectors the Messels were also keenly interested in the arts and this they expressed in their garden making. I do not know of any records that Gertrude Jekyll ever supplied plans for anything that was done at Nymans but she was friendly with the Messels and frequently visited them, as did the great William Robinson from his own home at Gravetye Manor not many miles away. The ideas which they were expressing must have met a very sympathetic hearing at Nymans and the Messels must surely have discussed their plans from time to time with both Miss Jekyll and Mr Robinson. There are certainly many features at Nymans which Miss Jekyll would have approved and I often wonder whether some of them were actually suggested by her.

Though the garden at Nymans is divided into numerous sections the design of these and their association is nothing like as tight and interlinked as at Hidcote Manor and Sissinghurst Castle. A plan of the garden shows no overall coherence, but as I have already remarked when discussing Hidcote, the plan is usually so different from what appears on the ground that it has little relevance to the impact a garden makes on visitors.

The features which most entitle Nymans to be included among the gardens of the outdoor decorators are the famous twin borders punctuated by elaborate topiary specimens, the terrace around the house and some of the features on the adjacent lawn, such as the 'basket bed' in which the basket, complete with handle is formed with winter jasmine and filled with growing hydrangeas, the old rose garden and the sunken garden over-looked by a stone loggia in the Italian style. In all these places plants are used with great discrimination to create carefully considered environments, each with a distinctive character of its own. The heather garden, made around a knoll at the southern end of the garden, starts beside an open lawn bounded by a raised walk and pergola, dripping with the long flower trails of wisteria as spring gives way to summer, and later edged with hydrangeas. On the far side of the knoll, the character of the heather garden changes completely, becoming much denser. A labyrinth of narrow paths winds between banks of heathers interspersed with many other shrubs – surely a splendid place for games of hide and seek by successive generations of Messel children.

Steps leading to raised walk and wisteria-covered pergola

Magnolia × loebneri
'Leonard Messel'

The herbaceous borders and the borders which form the back of the spring garden cross at right angles in a large, more or less rectangular area known as the Wall Garden. The Countess of Rosse says that the herbaceous borders were designed by her aunt under the tuition of Mr Robinson, so one may presume that they met with his approval. They are herbaceous only in the broadest sense of that word, meaning soft stemmed and not woody. Perennials, annuals and more or less tender bedding plants mingle in them as freely as they do in what we now call 'mixed borders', the one essential qualification being that each plant must make a positive contribution to the whole carefully orchestrated display.

That was what Miss Jekyll always advocated and one was as likely to find antirrhinums or dahlias in her border plans as delphiniums or phloxes. Even more remarkable for Robinsonian borders is the formality of the setting. A fountain of Italian design playing into a shallow stone basin on a pedestal is the centre piece where the spring borders cross the herbaceous borders and the wide path which separates them passes out of the Wall Garden beneath an elaborate Italian portico. And then, around the centre point, are those four topiary specimens of yew which by their size and elaborate sculpture dominate the whole of this area. They are shaped as massive drums each bearing a regal orb. Did Mr Robinson also approve these, after all his fulminations about formality? I am quite ready to believe that he did, for he seems to have been the least consistent of polemicists ever ready to contradict in art what he advocated in words. Did he not lay out his own forecourt at Gravetye Manor as a perfectly formal parterre with clematis-covered columns to accent its symmetrical pattern? Nothing could be less 'natural' though the planting was entirely in the spirit of the outdoor decorators.

The Wall Garden was an orchard before the Messels re-designed it with borders, and they left some of the trees to maintain a rustic air in the spring garden. Here daffodils, fritillaries and wood anemones grow freely in the grass. There are wide drifts of gentian-blue pulmonarias in the borders together with hyacinths and tulips. As a background among the fruit trees many flowering shrubs grow, together with ornamental trees including fine specimens of *Magnolia campbellii* and *M. sargentiana*. As a background at the house end is a lovely circular gazebo built of the local sandstone, surmounted by a conical roof and dovecot, and covered in camellias including the prodigal pink 'Donation'. It is one of the loveliest scenes in any English garden.

There are many other fine things at Nymans but they take us to other schools of thought regarding garden design, for there was nothing narrow about the Messel outlook. The extensive arboretum wraps around a paddock golden with daffodils in spring. It is, I suppose, really a collector's piece, full of good specimens but, since the Messels could not do anything without bringing art to bear upon it, the trees are so arranged that they make a wonderful blend of contrasting colours and shapes, some yellow, some grey, some blue and some green. A small white temple nestles among the trees at the highest point and there are superb views over the rolling Sussex countryside which seems to my eyes almost as composed as any landscape devised by Brown or Repton.

In what is known as the Top Garden, beyond the greenhouses and the
rose garden, are some of the finest specimen trees and shrubs including a
big plantation of magnolias, among which the delectable pale pink
'Leonard Messel' will be found. The planting here seems casual but I
suspect that it was, in fact, as carefully considered as everything else at
Nymans.

Falkland Palace Gardens

Whenever an ancient building has to be provided with a new garden a
problem of taste arises. Is the design to be a copy of some former garden (if
one existed), and if so at what period, for gardens seldom remain static for
long? Or should the garden be planned in the style of an earlier period
appropriate to the building, without reference to what was actually
there? Or yet again, would it be better not to attempt any reconstructions,
actual or imaginary, but instead to make a modern garden fitted for the
purpose for which it is required?

These were matters that had to be settled at Falkland Palace in Fife, in
1946, when restoration of that romantic hunting-palace of the Stuarts had
proceeded so far that the next logical step was to provide it with a suitable
setting. There were several sound reasons for the decision to make an
entirely new garden. Little was known about the gardens that had existed
there before, and no trace of them remained on the ground, which was
little more than a ploughed field used during the war years for the
cultivation of potatoes.

Certainly there were records of a lawn and garden as early as 1461, when Mary of Gilderland, Queen to James II of Scotland, lived there after her husband's death, and had a special door made in her apartment to give ready access to the lawn and garden. But whether this was the same great lawn that appears in a print of 1693 must remain very doubtful, for in Mary's time only the North Range of the Palace existed, and there was to be a great deal of building at Falkland during the intervening centuries.

So Major Michael Crichton Stuart, the hereditary Constable, Captain and Keeper of Falkland – which has always remained a royal possession – called in the garden architect, Percy Cane, let him see the print, and invited him to make an entirely new garden which would preserve a similar feeling of spaciousness. What Mr Cane produced was a thoroughly contemporary design which made considerable use of what he called 'garden glades'. Personally I think of these as formalised woodland, and if that seems a contradiction in terms, let me explain that in this kind of gardening an attempt is made to combine the orderliness of formal gardens with the free-flowing line and pictorial charm of the landscape style.

To achieve this union of apparently warring elements, trees, shrubs and herbaceous plants are massed informally in beds of irregular size and shape, surrounded by grass and disposed in such a manner that quite narrow paths open out into large open spaces. It is in fact just the kind of effect that one gets in woodland that has been partially cleared to form grassy glades and rides, but with the very important difference that, whereas the true woodland glade seeks to look as natural as possible, and to conceal the handiwork of the gardener or woodsman, this kind of garden makes no such pretence. Its lawns and grass paths are obviously well groomed, its verges are trimmed and sharp-edged, its soil cultivated and all its plants kept firmly in their place.

It is a kind of garden into which that most seductively artificial of all so-called 'natural' garden features, the herbaceous border, fits perfectly, and so it is no surprise to find that at Falkland Palace there are several fine examples, the largest of which extends for almost the whole length of the high stone wall forming the eastern boundary of the garden. This wall is itself well clothed with roses, clematis and other climbers, and over the years shrubs have replaced some of the herbaceous perennials, but to save labour rather than because, in this particular setting, they are more aesthetically satisfying.

Though the glade garden which Mr Cane made at Falkland is a complete entity, entirely satisfying in its own right and a great attraction to all visitors to the Palace, he was at pains to ensure that it emphasised the beauty of both the restored buildings and of the remaining ruins, and never competed with them for attention. He described his aims in 'The Creative Art of Garden Design' (published by *Country Life* in 1966), explaining how he planted columnar cypresses on the higher levels above the glade to accentuate what remains of the walls of the East Range.

To me, even more important than the vertical lines of these cypresses are the horizontal lines of the borders and grass paths on this side of the glade, which direct the eye unerringly to the most significant parts of the structure. I also admire the way in which he has used colour with the aim of giving delight without providing aggressive competition. These borders below the grey stone walls of the Palace are planted almost entirely in shades of blue, mauve and pink, with a few white flowers and silver leaves to liven the effect. It is all very beautiful, but in a soft, hazy way which leaves the building completely dominant.

The garden wall itself, and some of the foundations where they have no great architectural beauty, are covered with climbing or trailing plants, and one ragged buttress at the north-eastern corner of the range is completely smothered by a Russian vine (*Polygonum baldschuanicum*) which each summer erupts into a foaming torrent of creamy-white bloom.

In the long border against the eastern boundary wall much stronger colours are used, but since this border is separated from the Palace by the whole width of the glade and its surrounding beds, there is no competition between building and flowers.

Even before Mr Cane started to work at Falkland Palace, garden making had begun, but not on the ground level which we have been considering. High up above this, in the completely ruined North Range, a formal rose garden had been laid out following and emphasising the lines of the newly excavated foundations. This is a formal garden, its simple pattern accented by trimly clipped blocks of grey senecio and golden yew, and its beds filled with red and yellow roses, the royal livery colours of Scotland.

Mr Cane developed this idea by making a heather garden to mark the foundations of the old castle tower, and by planting pinks and other rock plants along the tops of some of the ruined walls. He also made steps to link these foundations gardens with the glade, and midway between the two, perched on top of the garden wall beneath the towering ramparts of the East Range, he laid out a long paved walk as a vantage point from which to survey the whole scene.

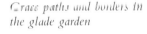

Grass paths and borders in the glade garden

In 1952 HM the Queen appointed, by charter, the National Trust for Scotland Deputy Keeper to Falkland Palace. The increased flow of visitors resulting from this development necessitated a few changes in the garden. A substantial reception centre, designed by W. Schomburg Scott, was built at the south end where the garden adjoins the main street of Falkland. To give ready access to the garden from this new building, Mr Cane made a flagged courtyard on two levels, ornamented with plants in Versailles tubs, and an immense stone draughts board with black and red draughtsmen. He also added a little railed terrace leading directly into the palace.

A little later, in 1955, the garden was completed with a feature suggested by Mr Euan Cox and designed by Mr Cane. This is a separate garden at the north end, beside the Royal Tennis Court which is said to be the only surviving real-tennis court (i.e. indoor court) to survive in Scotland from Stuart times.

This little garden contains two raised rectangular water basins, and is almost completely shut off from the main garden by high evergreen hedges. Just one wide opening has been left for access, and from this the most spectacular view of glade, palace and the backdrop of bare hills is obtained. From this extensive prospect one turns to a totally contrasted scene, enclosed and private, the high stone walls clothed with roses and clematis, white water-lilies floating in the pools, sweetly-scented phloxes surrounding beds, and slender Irish junipers standing like clipped topiary columns. It is a scene of almost medieval order and seclusion, and a fitting place in which to ponder on the turbulent history of this romantic building, and its present peaceful existence in such happily contrived surroundings.

Cranborne

Of what garden other than Cranborne in Dorset could it be said that an early 17th-century framework had to wait for a late 19th- and 20th-century filling? Some may disagree with this assessment, contending that by 1610 Cranborne already possessed a fully organised garden and that John Tradescant the elder made it. That is a story often repeated but the evidence is against it.

Tradescant is only known to have visited Cranborne once, in 1610, the proof being a payment of £2 2s 10d on November 10, 'To John Tradescent upon his bill of charges being sent to plant trees at Cranborne'. It is said that the trees were apricots, peaches, cherries and plums, and well they may have been for an orchard certainly was planted there.

Two plans exist, both said to be early 17th century, but neither dated or signed. Though they agree in broad outlines they differ in detail, one being simple and rather medieval in style, the other more complex and Renaissance in character. They may be the work of Mounten Jenninges, who was head gardener at Hatfield, or, in the more elaborate design, we may perhaps detect the hand of Robert Lyminge, clerk of the works at Hatfield, who was an excellent draughtsman. But this is pure conjecture. The one hard fact is that on October 17, 1609, Mounten Jenninges was paid £5 'to defray his charges to Cranborne being sent thither by our Honours appointment to survey the garden plot there'.

For a second positive reference to the garden we have to wait until 1685, when George Stillingfleet the younger, son of the Earl of Salisbury's agent at Cranborne, recorded that, 'There is no present tenant of the mansion house, nor hath been for many years past but it is kept for the immediate use of the now Earl of Salisbury as it was for his ancestors before him. And the lands which have lain about the house are two green courts north and

The blue border at Falkland Palace

*Rose-covered pergola at
Cranborne*

south, and two other plots east and west, designed as gardens but never
used as such, but encumbered with weeds, grass and thorny bushes, which
were long since beyond memory planted in several squares and other
figures and forms and a very old decayed orchard on the north side.'

To understand why a garden should be laid out, but never completely
planted, one has only to recollect the speed of events from the time that
Robert Cecil was created Viscount Cranborne in 1604. The following
year he was elevated to an earldom and very soon was exchanging
Theobalds for Hatfield and engaging on the great work of building and
garden making there. In 1612 he died, and though his son completed the
repairs and furnishings at Cranborne he never seems to have cared for the
place, or spent much time there. Nor did his successors, and so Cranborne
lay virtually unused until its beauty was re-discovered by the 2nd Marquess
of Salisbury and his family in 1863.

What they found remaining as garden were the four courts described by
George Stillingfleet and another at lower level to the east between house
and church, which was the original kitchen garden and was restored as
such. Each of the other courts was given its own distinctive character. Yew
hedges were planted around the west court, possibly on the lines of a
surviving hedge, and a bowling allée made at its northern end. All these
hedges have now grown to such a size that it is easy to imagine they have
been there since 1610. The sunken kitchen garden to the east was laid out
in rectangular beds and the walk above it to the church was backed by
yew, planted to form a series of rectangular niches. The north court was
already enclosed by walls, and twin herbaceous borders were made
through the middle of it to the wrought-iron gates, which lead to the
great avenue of Cornish elms that mark the original entrance to the
mansion.

Rosa '*Frühlingsgold*'

The south court, which was also enclosed by walls and the two gate houses, was given a simple oval of turf around which the new entrance drive circled. Here there was little planting except for a few Irish yews, standing like sentinels within the gates, and some climbing roses on the walls.

Photographs of the period show other borders of shrubs and perennials in various parts of the garden and make it clear that Cranborne rejuvenated had become a very pleasant place in which to live. It could have seemed sufficient, but in fact, so far as the garden was concerned, the work of restoration was only beginning. Some of the most important changes have been made by the wife of the late Lord Salisbury, and, since 1954, by the present Marquess and Marchioness, who came to the house while still Viscount and Viscountess Cranborne, and have completely transformed the garden.

Today it presents a perfect example of the art of outdoor decor with most of the enclosures already existing for over 300 years and only awaiting the skilful planting which has been so characteristic of much modern garden making in Britain.

The north court has become a white garden and the Victorian herbaceous plants in the central borders have been replaced by espalier-trained apple trees carpeted with single white pinks, chosen, as are so many of the plants at Cranborne, for their rich scent. Larger trees are loaded with the long stems of *Rosa moschata* 'Seagull', filling the air in summer with the perfume of its white flowers. There are shrub roses as well, 'Purity', 'Nevada', *Rosa alba plena* and Scotch briars among them, with lemon 'Frühlingsgold', apricot 'Buff Beauty', and old gold 'Rêve d'Or' to make the whites seem whiter still.

In the wide borders against the walls *Crambe cordifolia* expands its giant sprays of bloom like a mammoth gypsophila. There are many kinds of philadelphus, all scented, together with martagon lilies, valerian, poppies, foxgloves, abutilon, clematis and many other flowers all in white, with again discreet contrast from the buff-pink of *Bocconia cordata*.

Leaving this cool garden by a gate on the west side, one emerges into a much more colourful scene. *Genista cinerea* and Dutch honeysuckle embower the gateway in gold and russet pink, and below are peat beds filled with a variety of acid-soil plants, including gentians and celmisias, so often difficult to manage in warm southern gardens. More big borders by the walls are planted with daphnes, weigelas, peonies, both tree and herbaceous, *Hydrangea villosa*, more mock oranges, helianthemums, hardy geraniums and lots of roses, including *R. gallica complicata* with single pink and white flowers like huge dog roses.

The great court to the west of the house is open and uncluttered, used as a croquet lawn, with some fine beech trees on one side. Here there is only one elaboration, and it is discreet, a little parterre tucked away in the south-eastern corner of the court beneath the wall of the adjacent south court. It is just such a feature as appears in the more sophisticated of the two 17th-century plans, and is a graceful acknowledgment from the 20th century to those earlier planners whose designs were never fully executed.

Further to the west, beyond the croquet lawn, is the mount garden enclosed by high yew hedges with the bowling allée across its northern end. The mount itself is something of a mystery, for though it is frequently referred to it does not appear on either of the early plans. Perhaps it is a relic from an even earlier garden, which already by 1604 had become so eroded with age that it could be ignored. Certainly today it is nothing like the steep conical hill ascended by a spiral path which one sees in medieval illustrations of mounts. All that remains is a gentle swelling in the ground, which has been made into a notably three-dimensional parterre. The pattern is formed with eight box-edged beds; four long and narrow, set around the steepest part of the mount which is topped with a sundial, four much larger, shaped like truncated triangles, set at the outer corners of the garden. The narrow beds are entirely filled with lavender, the larger ones receive the cottage-garden treatment so typical of much of the planting at Cranborne, in which roses, many of them musk hybrids, rub shoulders with peonies, foxgloves, irises, sages and pre-Spencer sweet peas with the full old-time perfume. Yews, clipped to drum shape, are used to give height.

The greatest transformation in recent years has occurred in the south court, which has been completely changed from its original utilitarian aspect to a wonderfully pictorial delight. Its purpose as a forecourt has been retained by making a large paved rectangle in the centre, but this is elaborately patterned with insets of coloured pebbles to contrast with the stone slabs. There is a central sundial and various stone and terracotta pots and stone balls to accent the design, and the whole is contained within four simple L-shaped plots of grass. Borders under the flanking walls have the same deceptively casual planting, concealing so much art, which we have

Opposite: The walk from the church to the house

Below: New planting on the old mount at Cranborne

remarked elsewhere at Cranborne. Peonies predominate with lilies, including the apricot martagon, 'Mrs R.O. Backhouse', growing through them, and the walls are clothed in roses, including pink 'Madame Gregoire Staechelin' and the nearly forgotten crimson 'Souvenir de Claudius Denoyal'. Even the gate houses are swathed in pale pink roses ('New Dawn') and *Vitis coignetiae*, the leaves of which turn crimson in autumn.

Through a gate in the wall one can enter the walk to the church, now a flowery pilgrimage between borders lined with trained fruit trees and filled with annuals, biennials and perennials.

One can return via the old east court beneath a rose-covered pergola, between iris and lily-filled borders and along an avenue of pleached limes, to cross the entrance road, ascend a rough grassed rise and reach an entirely separate garden, a secret place the existence of which one would be unlikely to guess were one not told that it was there, since it is completely hidden by a wall and high hedges. Inside it is divided into three 'rooms', the first grassed, enclosed in beech and completely empty except for a statue. The second enclosure has a row of ornamental crab apples to one

The third and most secluded of the 'secret gardens' at Cranborne

side with peep holes to the outside world cut in its stout yew hedge. Beneath the high wall on the opposite side is a wide border filled with a variety of shrubs and perennials.

The third compartment is the most private of all, since one must pass through the other two to reach it. In this secluded place is to be discovered, more completely than anywhere else at Cranborne, that sympathetic understanding of the past which has made the garden restoration so out-standingly successful. This is an orderly garden, yet one in which every inch of space is used. Its beds, neatly edged in lavender cotton or chives, form a simple pattern which is both comforting and restful to the spirit.

Burford House

Burford House, a mile to the west of Tenbury Wells in Shropshire, is an austerely beautiful, red-brick house built in 1728. No doubt during its long history it has seen more than one fine garden, but when Mr John Treasure purchased the property in 1954 little trace of garden-making remained. There were some fine trees, including a towering wellingtonia and an elderly blue Spanish fir (*Abies pinsapo glauca*), relics, probably, of Victorian planting, and there was also a little summer house built like a classical temple which might well have been a feature in an 18th-century land-scape. The pediment is filled in with ironwork bearing the crest of the Bowles family, and it was William Bowles, proprietor of the prosperous Vauxhall Glass Works in London, who built the present house, though he never seems to have spent much time in it. But beyond these few relics of the past there was little but a large expanse of lawn in front of the house, and a still larger area of grass at the back where the garden is bounded by the River Teme and Ledwyche Brook which meet here. So, since there was so little to preserve, Mr Treasure was free to make whatever kind of garden he fancied.

He likes vistas, and thinks that they are most attractive when they curve so that there is always something round the corner to excite curiosity. So he started behind the house by marking out a series of large beds of irregular outline with the intention of providing himself with as many curving vistas as seemed reasonable in a garden of this size. So successful was he that he has never needed to alter greatly his original design, though he has extended it. But he says that in the early years he made plenty of mistakes in planting and spent much time moving things about, and trying new plants and new ways of grouping them.

I think that it is this care in selection and planting, as much as the overall design, which have made the Burford House gardens so supremely satisfying to the eye today. For Mr Treasure handles colour and leaf-form with as much care as Gertrude Jekyll did half a century ago, and he is just as ready as she was to use any plants to obtain the effects he wants. Shrubs rub shoulders with herbaceous perennials, roses, bedding plants, climbers, grasses and aquatics, and he seldom segregates any one type of plant in complete isolation from others.

He also makes use of another device which was a favourite with Miss Jekyll, the arrangement of groups with the tallest plants at each end instead of in the middle or at the back, as is more usual. In Mr Treasure's hands this often results in a dipping curve, so low in the centre that one can look right across a wide bed from one grass walk to another. This so greatly multiplies the possibility of creating further framed pictures that even Mr Treasure can find surprises.

Because of its very deep banks the river does not play much part in these views, though it is a pleasant feature in the landscape from the wide grass walk down the west side of the garden. But what the river does contribute to the garden is an inexhaustible supply of water for special features. The most spectacular of these is a canal in front of the house, a pool as uncompromisingly rectangular as the façade itself, for which it serves both as a setting and mirror. The pool is sparingly planted with water lilies so as not to cover its silver surface, and it stands centrally in a large lawn. This is flanked on each side by pump-fed streams, the banks of which are densely planted with a rich selection of moisture-loving plants.

At the back of the house another stream divides two of the vistas and is planted with similar generosity and imagination, while in complete contrast to these pseudo-natural conditions there is, towards the northeast corner of this garden, a circular pool set in a circle of paving and ringed with Irish yews.

Regular features such as this occur at several points in the garden, and it might be supposed that they would be an intrusion in what is mainly an irregular design. That this is not so is perhaps an indication of the folly of attempting to attach those overworked terms 'formal' and 'informal' to gardens of this modern type.

In a garden in which man is in such complete control there is nothing odd in finding that free-hand curves can give way to geometric figures, or that winding grass paths can be punctuated by paved areas, or that a change in level is negotiated by wide flights of steps flanked by handsome urns on substantial buttresses. This is a garden not a landscape, and the treatment is all of a piece, despite changes in manner necessary to meet particular needs.

Opposite: A little patio with a rectangular pool by the house

Below left: Clever colour planning using verbascum, artemisia, iris, stachys, lychnis and salvia

Below right: One of the artificial streams created at Burford House

Curving vistas between island beds at Burford House

It does not seem incongruous, therefore, to discover that, at the entrance to one of the largest and most open of the glades, a little rectangular area of paving has been made on which to stand a grey stone urn filled with foliage plants. Mr Treasure calls this his 'silver vase', for every plant in it has grey or silver leaves and there is a semi-circle of clipped yew to form a dark background to emphasise its silveriness. For those who are interested in creating a similar feature the plants used include *Senecio leucostachys, S. cineraria* 'Ramparts', *S. c.* 'Silver Dust' and *Helichrysum petiolatum.* Four dark-green columns of Irish yew surround this area, adding to its formality. They receive a little clipping plus encircling ties to keep them slim but they do not involve anything like the labour that would be necessary for common yew.

All the fine trees that existed when the property was purchased have been retained, and many more have been, and still are, being added. Particularly effective use has been made of columnar or spire-like trees such as the cypress oak, *Quercus robur fastigiata*, and numerous forms of Lawson cypress, including blue-grey *allumii*, dark green Kilmacurragh and *wisselii* (the latter evidently brushed down occasionally to rid it of the accumulation of dead leaves that can spoil its effect), grey-green *pottenii*, light green *erecta* and golden *lanei* and *stewartii.* Some are planted singly, some in small groups, to accent the design, and their trim shapes contrast almost as dramatically as topiary specimens with the billowy woodlands which form the southern horizon.

There are so many of these happy associations, and they change so much with the seasons, that I can only convey an impression by describing a few that I specially remember. There is, for example, the planting beside that wide western walk of masses of summer hyacinth, *Galtonia candicans*, with its broad strap-shaped leaves and stiff spikes of pendant, ivory white flowers, contrasted with the airy tussocks of the blue sheep's fescue grass, *Festuca ovina glauca.*

Then there are two of Mr Treasure's 'dipping curves' that come to mind; one in a rather dry, raised border in the south garden, the other beside one of the steams to the north of the house. The first starts at one end with grey and lavender *Buddleia* 'Lochinch', towering well above eye level, drops immediately to the mere 18 inches of *Erigeron* 'Elstead Pink', continues with orange-red *Phygelius capensis* and yellow, fern-leaved *Coreopsis verticillata*, and then climbs back to its starting height with cardoons and *Ceanothus* 'Gloire de Versailles'.

The group by the stream starts with the slender, waving stems of the wand flower, *Dierama pulcherrima*, bowed down by the weight of their purple flowers, and ends with the maize-like foliage of *Arundo donax* and the tall, umbrella-like inflorescences of the galingale, *Cyperus longus*. Between these heights spreads a purple carpet of *Astilbe simplicifolia atrorubens*, backed by a lovely green and cream striped reed, the name of which I do not recollect.

One could cite many more happy companionships, the gold of *Hypericum* 'Hidcote' intensified by the beetroot-red of *Cotinus coggygria* 'Royal Purple'; or purple clematis lying on a coppery-yellow carpet of *Calluna vulgaris* 'Robert Chapman'; or yet again pink *Penstemon* 'Evelyn' side by side with that good, non-flowering variety of lamb's ears, *Stachys lanata* 'Silver Carpet' and the South African blue daisy, *Felicia amelloides*, weaving its way among bushes of *Fuchsia* 'Rose of Castille Improved'.

Nor does Mr Treasure always work in soft colours as these random examples might suggest. When I was last at Burford House in July, there was one border that drew visitors from afar because of its rich colouring. It was planted almost entirely in reds, purples and magenta with silver for contrast, and the plants included *Potentilla* 'Monsieur Rouillard', an old and half-forgotten hardy perennial that looks like a coppery red geum; *Salvia superba*, always a winner; purple-leaved sumach, *Sedum maximum atropurpureum*, lavender cotton, *Artemisia* 'Lambrook Silver' and *Oreganum laevigatum*, a grey-blue marjoram elsewhere that I cannot recollect having seen before.

But in Burford House garden you take new plants and unexpected associations for granted and the real surprise would be if you failed to find them.

The 'silver vase'

Garinish Island

It was in 1910 that Mr Annan Bryce, a Belfast businessman, first perceived the potential beauty of a tiny, barren island in Bantry Bay on the south-west coast of Ireland near Glengariff, Co. Cork. Then little more than a rugged lump of blue shale, in part thinly covered with poor soil, it sustained nothing more than a little thin grass, heather and stunted gorse bushes. It was known as Garinish Island, which means the near island, because it lay only a few hundred yards from the shore near the village of Glengariff, and also as Ilnacullin, which means island of hollies, though it seems unlikely that holly could have survived unprotected in the teeth of

the Atlantic gales that sweep the bay. At the eastern end of the island, surmounting the highest outcrop of rock, stood a martello tower, more than 100 years old, but still in excellent repair. The only other indication of habitation was a ruined fort. Garinish Island had evidently seemed a good place to defend, but no one had ever considered it a desirable place of residence.

Mr Bryce had travelled widely and was interested in both gardening and architecture. No doubt he had seen many gardens made in unpromising places, though it seems unlikely that he could ever have encountered one quite so inhospitable as this. What it was that fired his imagination I do not know. Perhaps it was the wild beauty of the bay with its complex outline and many deep inlets. Maybe it was the wind-lashed sea and ever-changing sky, or the jagged background of the Caha Mountains, which look like crouching dinosaurs.

*The Italian Garden on
Garinish Island*

Whatever is was, he straightaway purchased Garinish Island and commissioned Harold Peto, then at the height of his fame as architect and garden maker, to plan him a house and garden. The house was to stand on the same rocky eminence as the martello tower, which, refaced and relined, would form part of it, so dominating the whole 37 acres, and the garden was to extend from this point to the western extremity of the island.

Work started on the garden in 1911, and for the next three years over 100 men were constantly employed in bringing soil and peat to make cultivation possible, planting great shelter belts of pine and cypress, building a high wall of the native blue shale to enclose a kitchen garden, laying a lawn and building a formal garden and pool with Italianate pavilions.

But though these were all features in a grand design intended to provide a setting for the house and to link it suitably with the wild landscape of Bantry Bay, the house itself was never built. Plans for it were prepared, and these are still displayed in the garden, but no stone of it was laid. The war intervened, the financial position changed, and before anything further could be done Mr Annan Bryce died in 1924.

For a few years his widow continued to maintain the garden, living in the cottage that had been built for the gardener, but in 1932 she decided to hand the work over to her son, Roland L'Estrange Bryce, a dedicated gardener who devoted himself enthusiastically to the task of completing the garden his father had begun. By this time the shelter belts had grown sufficiently to make the establishment of many exotic plants a possibility, and full advantage was taken of this, and the mild climate to build up a collection of impressive size and variety. But still no attempt was made to build a house, either to Mr Peto's original plans or to some more modest design.

I think this omission must be taken into account before it is possible to make a full assessment of the importance of this remarkable garden. An effort of imagination is required to surmount that rocky eminence with Mr Peto's Italianate villa, yet the effort must be made, for the one is an essential part of the other. Harold Peto, like his contemporary Sir Edwin Lutyens, was deeply concerned with the problems of uniting house and garden in one coherent scheme, yet with provision for a richness of planting not possible in the classical French and Italian gardens. This was to be a garden overflowing with the abundance of nature yet plainly displaying the dominance of man.

Garinish Island lies in Bantry Bay on the south-west coast of Ireland

Once this has been grasped everything at Garinish Island becomes logical. There is a strong central line leading from immediately below the hill with the martello tower to the far end of the island, where the formal garden repeats some of the features that would have been displayed by the main building. This line carries the eye onwards across the bay to the sharp cone of the Sugarloaf Mountain – the dominating feature of the landscape. The Italianate character of the villa that was never built is reflected in the clock tower and garden house at opposite corners of the kitchen garden, and the whole of this section is formal in conception, though it is a formality softened, and in part concealed, by generous planting.

But side by side with these central features of walled kitchen garden, rectangular lawn and Italian garden lies another, quite different garden, conceived in the woodland glade style. By skilful planting the natural contours of the island have been accentuated to suggest a long, deep valley traversed by a grassy glade and flanked by trees. At one end the valley is terminated by a great flight of steps, made of rough-hewn slabs of the local blue shale and leading up to the martello tower. At the other end a smaller, matching flight leads to a terrace from which further views of the bay and mountains are obtained, framed in the pillars of a small temple-like structure.

Every natural feature of the site has been exploited to serve the designer's purpose. At the lowermost point of the valley the dampness of the site has been used to form a water garden, backed by thick screens of bamboo and luxuriantly planted with aquatics and moisture-loving plants. Great outcrops of primeval rock flank this pool, extending almost across the glade and giving a sense of inevitability to the design, which no artificial rock construction could have equalled. Similarly the lawn garden, which separates kitchen garden from Italian garden, is flanked by steep outcrops of rock, which may well have been bared in places to make them more effective, but have certainly not been added to in any way. The transition from formal to natural is entirely unforced. The gardener, one feels, has simply made the best use of the natural resources of the site – until one stops to consider just how much art lies behind this apparent artlessness.

A book could be written about the trees and shrubs of Garinish Island. Even in the mildest Cornish gardens I have not seen more robust leptospermums, and these renew themselves freely from seed. The fine double-flowered variety 'Red Damask' is growing well in the Italian garden, where callistemons have attained considerable size and fascinate visitors with their scarlet bottle-brush flowers. Another shrub that puzzles and pleases a great many of the visitors who flock to Garinish Island in summer is *Desfontainea spinosa* with its absurdly holly-like leaves and masses of long tubular scarlet and yellow flowers.

Hoherias revel in the moist, mild climate and, like the leptospermums, regenerate themselves freely. As is to be expected, there is considerable variation in the seedlings, in both leaf form and flower size, and some forms of *H. sexstylosa* are particularly interesting, so far removed are they in character from what one regards as typical of that species.

Garinish Island is sometimes compared with Tresco in the Isles of Scilly. In so far as each is on a windswept island where gardening of any kind is

Desfontainea spinosa

rendered possibly only by massive windbreaks of evergreen trees, and each shares the warmth of the Gulf Stream Drift, the comparison is fair, but in almost every other respect it is misleading. Tresco enjoys a great deal of sunshine and has a moderate rainfall. Garinish Island rarely sees the sun for long and has an average annual rainfall of 70 inches. Few of the succulents which thrive at Tresco would survive in Bantry Bay, but rhododendrons and other evergreens revel in the moisture and there are even good specimens of that rare and difficult plant the Norfolk Island forget-me-not, *Myostidium nobile*.

Olearias are completely at home, as they are throughout the west of Ireland, and they are to be found at Garinish in unusual variety. One azara has reached a height of 30 feet or so, with a trunk like a sizeable birch. There are myrtles in plenty, *Myrtus luma* being particularly decorative with its cinnamon-coloured, peeling bark. Cestrums and nandinas thrive, as do embothriums, sophoras, grevilleas and tricuspidarias. *Drimys aromatica* has reached a great size, and in the valley garden *Dacrydium franklinii* weeps delicately alongside a stiffly-branched specimen of *Abies georgei*. This kind of happy association of contrasted plants is one of the features that keeps one constantly aware that someone with an eye for form as well as a knowledge of good plants has been at work on Garinish Island for many years.

In what was once the kitchen garden there are now twin borders lavishly planted with perennials, among them numerous species of watsonia.

By any standards this is a fine garden, even though it is an uncompleted masterpiece, sadly lacking the mansion to which it should have been the well-matched partner.

Mr Roland Bryce died in 1953 while on a visit to London and left the island to the President of the Irish Republic.

Crathes Castle

It is a somewhat astonishing fact that nearly all the great outdoor decorat-ors have been amateurs. Even Gertrude Jekyll started in that way and though she eventually worked for money she never really set up in business as a garden designer but used it more in the manner of a paying hobby. Of course, her principal collaborator, Sir Edwin Lutyens, was completely professional but he was an architect concerned with the structure of gardens and not at all with their furnishing and decoration which he was happy to leave to the competent judgment of Miss Jekyll.

Other women have been equally skilful though in the main they have confined their talent to their own gardens. Vita Sackville-West, at Sissinghurst Castle, has probably become the most renowned of these, but Lady Burnett of Leys proved at Crathes Castle that she had a similar mastery of the selection and arrangement of plants.

Burnetts had lived at Crathes, Banchory, Grampian since the 16th century and the garden seems to have been first laid out in the early 18th century. Probably it was then that the quite steep hillside on which the castle stands was terraced and it is said that the yew hedges, one at the end of the top terrace and the other dividing the second level like an enormous T laid across it, were planted in 1702. Certainly their great size today would lend colour to this story though it must not be forgotten that yew, once established, grows quite fast and that very substantial hedges and topiary specimens can be produced in as little as fifty years.

Certainly they were all there, much as they are today, when the Burnetts started to replant and remodel the garden in 1932. Sir James was keen on trees and shrubs and very soon amassed a notable collection including many species which might have seemed too tender for this part of Britain. Lady Burnett was more interested in herbaceous plants and it was her skill in associating plants of all kinds which made the garden so specially remarkable, probably one of the best half dozen of its kind in the British Isles.

What she did was very much what Lawrence Johnston had done nearly thirty years earlier at Hidcote and Sir Harold Nicholson and Vita Sackville-West were concurrently doing at Sissinghurst Castle, namely to divide the area into a number of more or less self-contained units. The main difference lay in the relative simplicity of the divisions which the Burnetts adopted: a series of rectangles not differing greatly in size and placed side by side to fill a much larger rectangle outside which the garden ceases to have any formal pattern and is planned in the manner of a landscape park. On paper it looks dull and obvious but on the ground it proves almost as satisfactory as the much more complex divisions of Hidcote and Sissinghurst Castle. For this, the great contrast in styles between one area and another and the always interesting, and sometimes quite inspired, plant grouping are responsible.

The original top terrace is now divided into two sections, one laid out in the manner of a Dutch garden with a small central pool surrounded by wall-like blocks of trimmed yew and simply-shaped flower beds, and the other mainly lawn closed in at the end by the largest and most spectacularly buttressed of the old yew hedges. What lifts the little pool garden far above the ordinary is the skill of the planting carried out almost entirely with perennial plants, both herbaceous and shrubby, and with a limited colour range in which purple, red and yellow predominate with great effect.

The same fastidious care in the use of colour is to be observed in all the

Ancient hedge of yew shelters a border at Crathes Castle

planting at Crathes. The second terrace, at a considerably lower level, was already divided into two more or less equal rectangles by the T-shaped hedges of yew. Both sections were laid out as parterres, each with its own symmetrical pattern of beds, but they do not match one another as they cannot be seen together because of the height of the intervening hedge. One is known as the Fountain Garden because its central feature is a fountain and this is planted largely in shades of blue with the annual echium much in evidence in summer and a fine paulownia as one of its most conspicuous trees. The second parterre is called a rose garden, though by no means all the beds are filled with roses and the central feature is a group of the large evergreen shrub, *Stranvaesia davidiana*, which has clusters of white flowers in summer followed by scarlet berries.

Tucked in between these two parterres and the top terrace is a narrow border in which some of the most tender shrubs grow. It always astonishes me that shrubs such as *Buddleia colvilei*, *Eucryphia glutinosa* and *Cornus nuttallii* can thrive at Crathes but thrive they do. No doubt the explanation is the shelter provided by the high walls and hedges coupled with the good air drainage on a sloping site which lessens the danger of damaging spring frosts.

Before moving down to the next level one can look down onto it from above and admire the economy of the means by which it has been divided into four more rectangles. The two great lines which strike across it at right angles are not formed with either walls of hedges but are paths passing between flower-filled borders. First there are twin borders of herbaceous perennials chosen mainly for their blue, mauve or pink flowers. In late summer it seems to be all Michaelmas daisies, yet an earlier visit will reveal delphiniums, campanulas, aconitums, hardy geraniums, eryngiums and many more kinds.

173

Herbaceous borders leading to the dovecot at Crathes Castle

The cross border is mainly white, but with a background of purple foliage and here there are many shrubs as well as herbaceous plants. From the higher level one cannot see beyond this, since a large mushroom-shaped Portugal laurel standing at the intersection of the borders blocks the view but when one reaches this spot it is revealed that more shrub borders complete the main axis.

Each rectangle has its own distinctive design and planting. One, known as the Camel Garden, is filled with island beds mainly for shrubs. A second, called the Trough Garden because its central feature is a well-planted stone trough standing beneath a large *Prunus serrula* with bark like polished mahogany, is surrounded by four triangular blocks of plants. A third is cut through diagonally by the most brightly-coloured borders in the garden in which peonies vie for attention with oriental poppies, lupins, flag irises and other gaily coloured flowers. Their purpose is to lead the eye irresistibly to the tall, peak-roofed dovecot which stands at the bottom corner of the garden.

The fourth rectangle, which was a utility plot when the Burnetts lived in Crathes Castle, is no longer required for that purpose by the National Trust for Scotland, which accepted the property and an endowment from Sir James, and has been effectively in control since 1962. So this final area has now been given a design and colour scheme which I think Lady Burnett would have approved. It is a lawn surrounded by wide beds of shrubs and herbaceous plants nearly all selected for their yellow or orange flowers or yellow or yellowish-green foliage, but with here and there just a touch of white to liven things up.

No verbal description can ever give much clue to the beauty of gardens such as this which rely almost exclusively on plants that are themselves constantly changing in appearance throughout the year. At one period it will be the giant lilies, *Cardiocrinum giganteum,* seen against the distant background of the castle and yew hedges which will most impress. At another the blue and pink herbaceous borders seen to dominate everything, and at yet another it will be the wonderful climbers on the walls that catch

Cardiocrinum giganteum

the eye, including what must be one of the finest specimens of *Actinidia kolomikta* in the kingdom. But at whatever season Crathes Castle is visited one cannot fail to be impressed by the skill and lavishness with which it has been planted.

Tyninghame

Tyninghame was purchased by the 1st Earl of Haddington in 1624 and has been in the possession of the same family ever since. It was, apparently, the 6th Earl (who succeeded to the title in 1681 and died 54 years later) who, with his wife's active help and encouragement, really started to improve the estate in a big way. Many of the trees he planted are still there, now grown into magnificent specimens. He it was who in 1706 planted the triple avenue of beech that extends eastwards the best part of a mile to the sea, and to the west of the house he used trees to form a 'wilderness', a fashionable feature of the period, though not at all the random arrangement the name might suggest. Straight paths and rides would have cut through the trees in a more or less regular pattern and some traces of these still remain, though time and changing tastes have nearly eliminated them.

*Tyninghame: Flora's Bower
surrounded by roses*

A wide grassed walk flanked by statues leads through the old kitchen garden

However a recent development, which perhaps consciously looks back to the past, is a new avenue of laburnums through the woodland, and when these have grown into a more or less continuous tunnel they will make a June feature as spectacular as the famous laburnum walk at Bodnant, Denbighshire.

There is, in fact, already a fully mature tree tunnel at Tyninghame, but that is of apples, and was planted about 100 years ago. It extends the whole length of the old kitchen garden outside one of the high brick walls which completely enclose it.

As so often in Scottish gardens this kitchen garden is a long way from the house, separated from it by woodland and shrub borders, and it probably always served a partly ornamental purpose. Photographs taken in 1902 show twin herbaceous borders running right through the middle of it with a handsome stone doorway at one end bearing the date 1666 and leading out into the apple tunnel, and at the other end terminated by a little parterre with four 'knots' cut in box beneath a conservatory terrace. Gate and box parterre still remain, but the borders have been grassed over, the yew hedges that backed them have been encouraged to grow much higher and used as a background for statues, so converting the whole into an impressive allée in the French manner, which looks splendid and requires little maintenance. It is one of the many changes which the present Countess of Haddington made after she took charge of the garden in 1952.

In another section of the kitchen garden a good collection of trees, shrubs and roses has been made by Lord Haddington, partly in island beds, partly in the sheltered borders beneath the old walls. The climate at

Tyninghame is surprisingly mild, thanks to the proximity of the North Sea, and this, with a modest 24 inch annual rainfall, permits the cultivation of many plants that might seem tender for an east-coast Scottish garden. A useful collection of eucalyptus is growing fast, yellow and white Banksia roses flower well, and other unexpected exotics include *Drimys winteri*, *Robinia kelseyi*, *Clerodendrum trichotomum*, Italian cypress and *Cercidiphyllum japonicum*.

But the greatest delights at Tyninghame are around the mansion itself. This is in the Scottish baronial style, built of mellow red stone, with plenty of turrets, stepped gables and tall chimneys. Most of the building dates from 1828 when the old house was extensively altered and enlarged by William Burns.

The drive is to the north and the garden is completely screened from it. Visitors enter a large parterre to the east of the house. Old photographs show this filled with a typically elaborate Victorian bedding scheme, but now the pattern is much simpler, with large beds filled with white and yellow roses, chiefly 'Iceberg' and 'King's Ransom'. In the centre is one of those many-faced sundials that seem to abound in Scotland, this one said to have been copied in 1800 from a much older original. The whole conception is dignified without being in the least pompous, and in the corner an amusing little pink garden house in the Strawberry Hill-Gothic manner guards the entrance to what I regard as the greatest achievement at Tyninghame and the one that really puts it in the front rank of 20th-century plant gardens.

This is a small garden so completely shut off from the rest that it has the surprise quality of an Italian *giardino segreto*. Once upon a time it was a tennis court, but it had been abandoned for so long that when Lady Haddington decided in 1956 to make it her very own garden it was little more than a hayfield. Now it drips with roses, many of them old varieties chosen for their soothing colours and sweet perfumes, but they are not segregated like the modern roses on the terrace, but mingle contentedly with all manner of other flowers. Red and white striped 'Rosa Mundi' finds agreeable companionship in purple *Geranium dalmaticum*, and the York and Lancaster rose is paired with the purer colour of *Geranium* 'Johnson's Blue'. The highly distinctive quartered flowers of 'Queen of Denmark' gain added beauty from the harmonising pinks, with contrasting flower shapes and foliage colours of 'Celestial', 'Constance Spry', 'Pink Moss', 'Ville de Bruxelles' and 'Empress Josephine' with 'Golden Clarion' hybrid lilies in close attendance. A wide arch, heavy with the bloom of rose 'Bourbon Queen' and *Lonicera halliana*, frames a view of grey and lavender *Buddleia fallowiana* and blue delphiniums; *Campanula* 'Loddon Anna' is grouped with *Linum perenne* and such good roses as 'Reine des Violettes', 'Bloomfield Abundance' and 'Aloha'. That loveliest of martagon lilies, apricot 'Mrs R.O. Backhouse', thrives beneath the showering sprays of *Rosa filipes*, and yet another group consists of roses 'Golden Wings', 'Fritz Nobis', 'Nymphenburg' and 'Penelope'.

Statuary at Tyninghame

So one could go on more or less indefinitely, for this garden is crammed with felicitous plant associations. Flora presides over the scene from a central treillage bower surrounded by yet more roses, and at one end a little pool set in the wall might seem to be a wishing well for those visitors desperate to catch the gift of using plants so well.

There are many other fine things at Tyninghame, though none quite so rare as those in this secret garden. In a sheltered courtyard on the south side of the house stands an old Venetian well-head surrounded by many interesting plants including *Hydrangea villosa*, *Solanum jasminoides*, *Senecio hectori*, pink, scented climbing jasmine (*Jasminum stephanense*), and myrtle grown from a sprig of the posy of one of Queen Victoria's bridesmaids.

Wide, curving borders of herbaceous perennials, shrubs and roses have been made below the south terrace wall.

The terrace continues to the east in an even more informal development of island beds and borders known as the Grove. Here lawns and grass paths provide long and constantly changing vistas. There is a good collection of sorbus species, and there is also a heather garden with rare pines, including Mexican *Pinus patula*, with the most slender of needles, as well as celmisias and the Chatham Island forget-me-not, *Myostidium nobile*, which thrives on a diet of seaweed, plentifully available on the silver strand of Ravensheugh Sands, little more than a mile away.

It is further evidence, if any were needed, that this is a garden in which the cultivation of plants is as well understood as their happy association.

Opposite: View of Snowdon across the Italian terraces at Bodnant

Right: The little parterre with box 'knots' in the old kitchen garden at Tyninghame

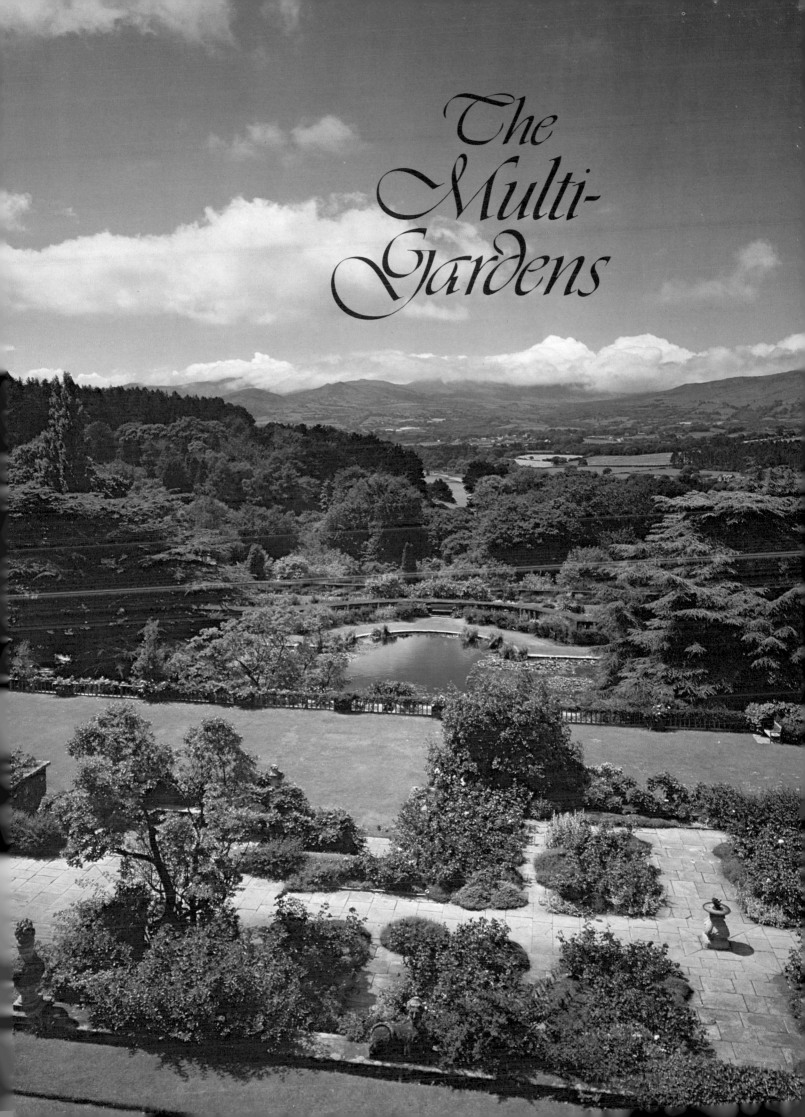

The Multi-Gardens

A detail of the magnificent rock garden at Wisley in Surrey

There are gardens which cannot be assigned any particular period or style. Some, such as Chatsworth and Hampton Court, are very old but have developed with the passing centuries, acquiring new features to satisfy the fancies of successive generations or owners. They might be regarded as living encyclopaedias of changing fashions and it is astonishing how well these often associate so that one is scarcely aware of them until the anachronisms that inevitably exist are pointed out by experts.

Others, like Lochinch and Sheffield Park, are old gardens that have been given entirely new planting which has changed their character radically, some would say for the better and some for the worse. And there are others, of which Bodnant is an outstanding example, with owners so eclectic in taste that they happily borrowed from many periods and styles to produce the effects they required.

There are also among these multi-gardens, as I have called them for want of any accepted name, a few that were consciously made to exhibit as many styles as possible. One of the most notable examples is the garden of the Royal Horticultural Society at Wisley, to which a canal pool and formal walled garden were added a few years ago, not because they were considered essential to the overall design but because, until that time, the garden had lacked any formal features. Since Wisley is maintained for the pleasure and instruction of the RHS members the Council decided that it should be made as representative as possible of all garden styles.

Harlow Carr near Harrogate is also constantly accepting new features to make it more interesting to its owners, the members of the Northern Horticultural Society. On a much smaller scale, Compton Acres at Poole was planned in nine separate sections, each representing a different period or style of garden making. Its creator, Thomas William Simpson, surrounded his house with what he regarded as a typically English garden and in a circle around this and at a slightly lower level made a Roman garden, a Japanese garden, an Italian garden, a palm court, a heather and rhododendron dell, a rock and water garden, a herbaceous garden and a memorial garden for his son.

It cannot be wholly without significance that these multi-gardens include some of the most popular in the country. Purists may deplore them as having been despoiled or being no more than pastiche, but the garden visiting public loves them and visitors flock to them in tens of thousands. It is easy to sneer at the low level of public taste. It might be more sensible to look more closely at these gardens and discover why it is that so many of them are genuinely beautiful.

Chatsworth

Sir Joseph Paxton

If one had to assign a dominant style to the garden at Chatsworth it would be Victorian because it was in the middle of the 19th century that it acquired a great many of the features which remain today. Joseph Paxton came to Chatsworth in Edensor, Derbyshire as head gardener in 1826 and despite his many other activities which included the design of the glass building in Hyde Park for the Great Exhibition of 1851, its subsequent removal to south London to become the Crystal Palace and the planning of numerous public parks, he remained at Chatsworth until 1858 by which time he and the 6th Duke of Devonshire had largely remodelled the garden.

Yet for all their industry and innovation much remained from earlier periods of garden making. Most spectacular of these and still a prime attraction to visitors is the great cascade or water staircase part of the great formal garden laid out for the 1st Duke of Devonshire towards the end of the 17th century. The 'staircase' itself was designed by a Frenchman, Grillet, said to have learned his craft under André Le Nôtre but the lovely Cascade Temple which stands at the head of the cascade was not added until a few years later and was probably designed by Thomas Archer, also the architect of the pavilion which terminates the long canal at Wrest Park.

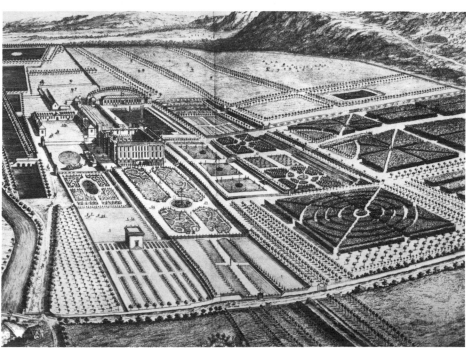

Knyff's engraving of the gardens of Chatsworth in 1699

Some other features from this 17th-century garden survive including the elaborate Seahorse Fountain which plays into a circular pool midway between the Canal Pool, made in 1703, and the south front of the mansion.

It was certainly natural that, nearly a century later, Lancelot (Capability) Brown should be called in to remodel part of the garden in the fashionable landscape style. However this was not a major commission for Brown and the changes he made were not of such a sweeping nature as in many other places. Most of the London and Wise garden had probably already disappeared, the west front of Chatsworth, probably the work of Thomas Archer, was being cleared so that it might become the front instead of, as previously, the back of the building and Brown was largely concerned with improving the prospect on this side. This he did by raising the level of the River Derwent, improving its line and laying out the surrounding land as a pleasantly wooded park. The Cascade and the Seahorse Fountain remained untouched.

*The wall cases at Chatsworth
designed by Paxton*

Paxton and the 6th Duke of Devonshire worked unceasingly yet they too left some of the old features and interferred little with Brown's work. They planted an arboretum, erected some theatrical rock work and constructed a large reservoir on the hilltop behind Chatsworth to supply a fountain which they placed at the mansion end of the old Canal Pool. So great was the flow of water from this reservoir that it could throw a jet 290 feet high. It was called the Emperor Fountain because it was installed especially for an expected visit by the Czar of Russia, but he never came and it is the public who today benefit most from the duke's extravagances.

Above all Paxton built highly original and effective glasshouses, some of which also remain. Visitors can still see the ingenious glass cases which he built against the high south-facing wall which forms the northern boundary of the garden.

The new plant house

It was a tragedy for Chatsworth and for British horticulture that Paxton's finest creation at Chatsworth, the Great Conservatory, which took four years to construct and was well ahead of its time both in design and its iron structure, had to be demolished in 1920 owing to serious neglect during the First World War. Its fame on its completion in 1840, eight years before the Palm House at Kew, was so great that a special railway station was built to receive the tens of thousands of visitors who flocked annually to Chatsworth to admire it. It was in the great glasshouse that the giant water lily, *Victoria regia*, flowered for the first time in Britain.

For all these reasons it is particularly fitting that Chatsworth should again be in the vanguard of horticultural progress with the first greenhouse to be constructed in a privately owned garden on a principle that has only once before been used for this kind of structure anywhere in the world. Its forerunner was the great plant house at the Royal Botanical Garden, Edinburgh, which was completed in 1967 and has won a Civic Trust Award. G.A. Pearce was the architect of both houses, and he describes his aims as being to create enclosed environments within which plants can be grown and displayed in a natural way, unhampered by drips due to condensation, structural shading or obstruction from internal supports.

The stability of both houses depends on an interaction between thin portal frames and an external suspension system which takes much of the weight of the main structural members. The Chatsworth glasshouse is 110 feet long and 40 feet wide and is divided internally into three sections to permit divergent environmental conditions to suit different types of plants. The minimum height at the eaves is 10 feet and at the ridge 20 feet, but since the house is placed on sloping land these heights are considerably exceeded in the western section, which is at a much lower level and is entered from the middle section down curving flights of steps. This is the warmest environment of the three and here a large pool has been constructed so that *Victoria regia* can flourish once again at Chatsworth as it did in Paxton's day.

It may be wondered why a sloping site should have been selected, and why the greenhouse should run east to west when north to south is generally recommended as giving a more even distribution of light. The explanation is that the site has been carefully chosen both to prevent any possibility that the new structure would obtrude on any of the views from the lawns and parterres adjacent to Chatsworth House and to fit into what might be called a 'greenhouse precinct', bounded to the south by the old Camellia House, built for the 1st Duke of Devonshire about 1700, and to the north by Paxton's glass cases and a vinery of the same period. In fact this conception has come off splendidly, there is complete unity between the whole group of buildings and because of the way in which they are placed amid trees and shrubs, which screen without shading them, none in any way detracts from any of the others.

Particularly fortunate was the discovery of an old archway in the middle of the Camellia House that at some period had been filled in, but has now been re-opened to provide a delightful vista from the flagged terrace at the west end of the new glasshouse through the Camellia House, across the central path of the rose garden and on over the wide lawns below the Great Cascade to the Serpentine Walk, planted by the present Duke in 1953, which leads to the bust of the 6th Duke of Devonshire, who presided over Chatsworth in Paxton's day. Because this is a picture seen through an archway it is a one-way view, linking the new greenhouse precinct firmly with the old garden while revealing virtually nothing of that precinct in return.

The famous cascade at Chatsworth

Wallington

The 1st Duchess of Northumberland, after visiting Wallington in about 1750, reported that the garden was very extensive and contained a great number of plantations 20 years old and a kitchen garden with a stove in it, as well as a Vaux Hall and a very expensive Chinese building. But, she concluded, 'It is not laid out in a pretty Taste'. Since we have no record of what her taste in gardens was we may leave this judgment aside while being grateful for even this tiny piece of evidence about what was happening then at Wallington. For this was undoubtedly one of the peak periods of garden making there, when great changes were undertaken and the whole place was being converted from almost barren wasteland, fit only for hunting, to the carefully planned and well-wooded estate we know today. Yet for all the activity, spread probably over a period of nearly half a century, with great expenditure of money, surprisingly little is known of what actually happened in the garden, though a great deal is known about what was done to the house.

The story probably begins in 1728 when Sir Walter Calverley Blackett inherited Wallington from his uncle, the second Sir William Blackett. At that time the Blacketts resided at Newcastle and used Wallington more or less as a hunting lodge. Sir Walter determined to make it his principle residence and immediately set about the improvement of the whole place.

One of the popular local stories is that at one stage he engaged the assistance of the most famous of local heroes, Lancelot (Capability) Brown, who was born in 1716 at Kirkharle, little more than a mile to the south of Wallington. When he grew too old for the little school there, he continued his schooling at Cambo, less than a mile to the north. Then, his schooldays over, he was engaged as a gardener by Sir William Lorraine at Kirkharle Hall and remained in his service until 1739 when he went south. He must, therefore, have been well aware of the changes that were being made at Wallington, but that he would be consulted while only a junior gardener seems unlikely.

However, local tradition does not claim that Brown, the garden boy, planned any part of Wallington, but that he returned about 1766 at the height of his powers and fame to express views about what should be done. It may be so, for meanwhile his brother had married a daughter of Lorraine of Kirkharle, but there is no documentary evidence to prove it nor any sign of Brown's highly distinctive style at Wallington, though it can perhaps be seen in the great lake at Rothley, a few miles to the north, which also belonged to the Blacketts.

What seems certain is that a plan was prepared for Sir Walter very soon after he came to Wallington, probably not later than 1735. There are no records as to who prepared it, but the style is reminiscent of Bridgeman and Kent, who had many imitators. Nor have we any means of telling how much of this plan Sir Walter executed. There is now little trace of the very elaborate design shown to the west of the house, though something of the kind certainly did exist there and was probably not swept away until the 19th century. The plan shows a serpentine 'river' or canal starting near the

A rock-lined stream runs through the walled garden at Wallington

west of the house, turning northwards and then eastwards to join the main avenue some distance north of the house. It also shows two large pools to the west, one roughly U-shaped and described as 'a piece of Water to be made to humour the Ground and lies 20 feet below the level of the Terras', and a rotunda placed at the west end of this same terrace.

All have now disappeared but the two lakes shown to the east of the house are still there. One, curling from north to south in the shape of a horn, is now known as the China Pond because a pavilion in Chinese style, presumably the 'very expensive Chinese building' described by the Duchess of Northumberland, once stood beside it. Alas, all trace of this building has long since disappeared, though there is a drawing at Wallington which possibly depicts it. The second pond is still farther to the east, roughly in the form of a meat chopper, described on the plan as 'a piece of Water not to be seen from the House'. The rectangular plots above it are the Kitchen Garden, and the tiny rectangle in the wall which bounds it on the north is 'a Building for use of the Gardener'. The kitchen garden disappeared long ago, when this portion was remodelled in the 1760s, and is now woodland, but the handsome pillared portico to the very unpretentious little cottage behind remains and has been well restored.

One of the four dragon heads

Of the present day 'garden' – the walled garden which is Wallington's major attraction today for flower lovers – there is no trace at all on the plan. It lies still farther to the east in the little valley which can be seen in the plan curling away southwards and through which the stream which feeds the China and Garden Ponds discharges its water into the Wansbeck, flowing round the southern perimeter of the estate. Yet this garden is also 18th-century in character and seems to belong to the same period of planning as the rest. It is completely shut off by a high wall. The north side of the little valley has been built up as a deep terrace retained by a high stone wall and was obviously designed for glasshouses and other buildings. One of these remains, an elegant two-storey potting house or bothy built in the manner of a pavilion and surmounted by a stone owl, a recurring symbol at Wallington, for it is the Calverley crest.

At the extreme east of this garden is a small but well built house, also of 18th-century origin, for which many attractive drawings exist. Arthur Young in his *Northern Tour*, published in 1771, records that a new kitchen garden and gardener's house had been made at Wallington.

Today the visitor's first impression of Wallington, after he has crossed the elegant stone bridge over the Wansbeck, built in 1760 to the design of James Paine, will be of four grinning stone dragon heads set out on the lawn above the ha-ha which separates it from the road. They came in Sir Walter Blackett's time as ballast in coal ships returning empty from London to the Tyne, but they were originally used at Rothley Castle and were only placed in their present position in 1928.

The portico of the old cottage built into the kitchen garden wall seen from the lower pond

Lead figures from the terrace wall

The garden around the house is conventional and on the whole un-remarkable, though it makes a very pleasant setting to the mansion. There are plenty of good trees, including some new ones planted since the National Trust took over the management of Wallington in 1958. There are also some particularly well-stocked flower borders, at their best in summer. The views from the lawn are pleasing, over rolling Northumbrian country, and are particularly extensive towards Hadrian's Wall nine miles to the south.

The woodland garden to the east is separated from this home garden by the road leading to Cambo and Rothley. Many of the trees are very old and considerable thinning has been necessary. Paths wind through the trees, one leading northwards to the China Pond, another running eastwards to divide around the Garden Pool, now filled with brandy-bottles (*Nuphar luteum*) and fringed with flag irises, water plantain and loosestrife, and eventually to reach the high wall which cuts out all view of the 'new garden beyond'. On the way the visitor will see to the left, at the head of an avenue through the trees, the Portico Wall, so named because of the quite elaborate portico over the little cottage built into the wall, and may turn aside to examine it more closely, for it is an attractive as well as an historic feature. There is considerable replanting here too, full use being made of the sheltered south-facing wall for climbing plants, and the whole of the woodland is being enriched with under planting of rhododendrons and other shade-loving shrubs.

But it is not until the visitor has passed through the solid doorway of the walled garden that the full delight of garden making at Wallington over the past century will burst into view. Here the story can be recorded in full since it is very largely the work of one man, Sir George Otto Trevelyan, who in his notebook kept an almost daily record of what he was doing. He inherited Wallington in 1879 and, like his ancestor Sir Walter Blackett, set about improvements at once. He continued for nearly 50 years, until his death in 1928 at the age of 90.

The garden is unusual in many respects and its individuality stems in part from its metamorphosis from mainly utilitarian to largely pleasure use. The site is awkward in shape and contour, lacking any parallel sides, with a two-way slope and a continuous curvature towards the south. One of the few perfectly straight lines is provided by the high terrace wall on the north side – the same wall that was first made in the mid-18th century, though largely rebuilt by Sir George in 1902.

Here it was apparently possible to retain a few of the original plants, building the new house around them and so enabling them to grow on unchecked. It certainly contains some magnificent specimens, though not all are as old as this. A huge lemon verbena (*Lippia citriodora*) is said to be pre-1903, but the enormous fuchsias were planted later. Perhaps some are referred to in a note for 1908 in which Sir George says that 'the winter garden was furnished from Olivotti's and creepers planted. A great success.' A specimen of *Fuchsia* 'Rose of Castille Improved' has an almost tree-like trunk 27 inch in diameter near the base. There are other fuchsias almost as big, but known to be younger, and also a very large, richly scented heliotrope which, like the fuchsias, goes right up to the rafters.

Flower borders at Wallington spanned by rose-covered arches

The terrace wall is adorned with enchanting lead figures which were first obtained for the Blackett house in Newcastle. It has been suggested that they are of Dutch origin, but such figures were being made in England throughout the late-17th and 18th centuries by Van Nost, Cheere and others, and it must not be overlooked that the Blacketts had interests in lead as well as in coal. The figures are very varied, including a squire, Scaramouche, folk dancers, Grecian goddess, Roman gladiator and soldier.

From the terrace there is an almost aerial view of the little curling, slanting garden in the valley below and it is sufficiently high to permit one to see right over the far wall and across the meadows to Paine's bridge by which we entered the demesne. In this valley Sir George planted opulent flower borders, made rockeries and laid out a lawn without interfering with the natural contours of the land.

One development of importance since Sir George's day is a kind of rustic terrace made at the west end of the garden by Mary, Lady Trevelyan, in 1938. This is really a viewing platform for the whole garden, sheltered by a semi-circular wall with wide flights of steps sweeping down on each side. The overflow from the Garden Pool is piped to this terrace to feed a little pool from which it is channelled into a rocky stream pursuing a sinuous way across the lawn until it disappears underground in a considerable sunken rock and water garden about a third of the way along its length. This feature has been further developed by Graham Thomas working for the National Trust, the stream now reappearing farther down the lawn to flow again between rocky banks, thickly planted, like those higher up, with violas, campanulas, primulas, astilbes and many other plants that maintain a good display for much of the spring and summer.

Other changes have been made in recent years. There is now a new flower border down the south side of the garden where formerly there was a cart road. At the far end of the lawn twin borders have been made behind a new yew hedge and planted mainly with blue and yellow flowers. They are spanned by metal arches clothed with yellow roses and this covered way terminates at its lower end in a large, flagged circle, also enclosed in yew. The lower part of the lawn has been planted, orchard fashion, with small flowering and ornamental trees, shrubs and shrub roses.

Sir George's great herbaceous border below the terrace wall has been replaced by a much narrower border used largely for climbing roses, but the rocky edge of the old border beside the path has been retained and is well clothed with vigorous and free flowering rock plants, the intervening space between edging and wall border now being mown grass.

Shrub roses and other flowering shrubs and perennials are used to fill the corners beside Lady Trevelyan's rocky terrace and a similar style of mixed planting is followed in the narrower border along the top terrace. The bottom of the garden, once reserved for vegetables, is now covered in mown grass, the handsome wrought iron gates in the high brick wall are revealed and a pool with formal cascade and some good surround planting has been added. The result of all these alterations is a garden requiring considerably less maintenance, yet still full of colour and interest from spring to autumn.

Lochinch and Castle Kennedy

To understand this garden of Lochinch and Castle Kennedy one must know a little about its history, and that takes one back nearly 300 years. The story begins with John Dalrymple, born in 1673, who became 2nd Earl of Stair on the death of his father in 1707 and received Castle Kennedy as part of his inheritance. He distinguished himself both as a soldier and as a diplomat, was a prominent Whig politician and did much to improve agriculture in Scotland. Under Marlborough he was rapidly promoted from aide de camp in 1703 to major-general in 1709. He fought with valour in all Marlborough's campaigns and left the army with him in 1711 when the Tories came to power.

Despatched in 1715 as minister plenipotentiary to Paris, he was made ambassador after the death of Louis XIV and took a leading part in the diplomatic events of that period. Unhappily his lavish spending dissipated much of his fortune, and in trying to recoup his losses he fell out with his fellow Scot, Law, Minister of Finance in Paris, and was recalled. For the next 20 years he resided mainly in Scotland, spending much of his time at Newliston near Edinburgh, where it is said he laid out the grounds to represent the disposition of troops at Blenheim. George II made him a

Plan of the gardens at
Castle Kennedy and
Lochinch

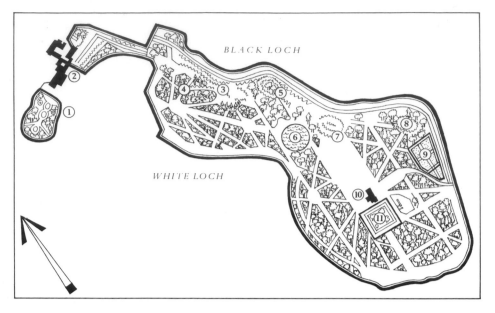

field marshal in 1742, and he fought under the king's command at Dettingen, but retired at his own request the following year. He died in 1747.

During all this period we hear little of Castle Kennedy, which was remote from the centres of government and command that the earl was accustomed to frequent. The castle, built in the early 16th century, is a couple of miles east of Stranraer. It stands on a ridge on a mile-long isthmus between two freshwater lakes, the White Loch to the south west and the Black Loch to the north east, beyond which well-wooded hills rise towards the Wigtown Moors.

On this wild and irregular site the 2nd Earl of Stair created a garden on a grand scale, though precisely when he did this and what manner of garden he made we do not know. Some think he started work as soon as he inherited the property, but this seems unlikely since he was then campaigning with Marlborough. Others believe it was between 1720 and 1740, when he would certainly have had ample opportunity; yet Castle Kennedy had been destroyed by fire in 1716, so why should he expend a great deal of money and labour in making a garden around a ruin? A third possibility is that much of the work was done after 1742.

In his letter of resignation after Dettingen he asks the king to 'give me leave to return to my plough without any mark of your displeasure'. This George II did, appointing him Colonel of the Inniskilling Dragoons in 1743 and Colonel of the Scots Greys in 1744, and tradition says that these regiments were used to make the garden. The principal avenue from Castle Kennedy to the White Loch is called Dettingen Avenue, which may be a clue, but it is all no more than conjecture. What is certain is that the earl shaped the natural contours of the isthmus into a series of terraces, so bold in their outlines that time has been unable to blur them. Mount Marlborough is the highest of them – a sugarloaf hillock made to look much bigger than it is by a top knot of large trees. Close at hand is the Terraced Mound or Guardsman's Bonnet, completely bare except for turf and cut into a series of curving terraces overlooking a circular pool at the lowest part of the isthmus. The effect here is of a large amphitheatre, and it is from this point that the finest views can be obtained of the old castle. A long, flat-topped embankment, the Giant's Grave, flanks the Black Loch beyond Mount Marlborough and connects with other level walks from which ever-changing views of lakes, countryside and gardens can be obtained.

The 2nd earl seems also to have made the canal across the isthmus at its south-easterly end, thereby, perhaps, draining a bog and certainly allowing uninterrupted flow of water from the White Loch to the Black Loch and thence to Loch Ryan.

Tradition has it that the original garden was in the French manner, with a formal pattern of allées criss-crossing through the trees, but there is no firm evidence of this. However, when, about 1840, the gardens began to be restored by the 8th earl it was to a formal pattern that he worked. At this time there was still no residence at Castle Kennedy. When the family wished to be in Galloway they lived in Culhorn Barracks a few miles to the south. Not until 1864 was the building of the new house, Lochinch Castle, begun at the north-western end of the isthmus, but by then the new garden was already growing up. There is an old plan that shows a pattern of allées covering much of the ground and several quite elaborate parterres between Castle Kennedy and the White Loch. The allées or avenues remain, though some are now blocked or blurred by a century and more of unrestricted growth, but of the parterres there is no trace; only a walled garden immediately behind the castle and Dettingen Avenue, a wide grassed ride between huge holm oaks, leading to the lakeside.

Overleaf: View of Castle Kennedy Top right: View across the Round Pound to the White Loch

Below: The Guardsman's Bonnet or Terraced Mound

The time could not have been more propitious. Exotic plants were pouring into Britain from many parts of the world. From 1840 until his death in San Francisco in 1863 William Lobb was collecting for Veitch of Exeter, first in South America, from which he sent quantities of good seed of *Araucaria araucana*, the monkey-puzzle tree, and later in western North America, where he collected many fine conifers. In 1847 Dr Joseph Hooker was starting the series of expeditions into the Himalaya that were to increase so greatly knowledge of rhododendrons.

From all these sources, and no doubt from many others, seeds or plants came to Castle Kennedy. They could hardly have come to a better place, for the climate of Galloway is mild and moist, and that is precisely what many of these new trees and shrubs required. By 1860 the head gardener at Castle Kennedy was giving, in *The Scottish Gardener*, an enthusiastic account of the monkey puzzle. 'As an ornamental tree,' he wrote, 'the araucaria is very greatly used and is much and justly admired in localities where it grows freely.' By 1905 Elwes and Henry could record that the largest of these araucarias was 50 feet high, and at the Royal Horticultural Society's Conifer Conference in 1931 George Clark estimated the trees as 87 years old.

The rhododendron seeds sent by Hooker did equally well. The slightly tender tree rhododendrons (*Rhododendron arboreum*), many of them planted beside the carriage road that nearly encircles the Black Loch, liked it so well that many reproduced themselves and interbred with other species. Under the care of the garden-loving 10th earl, who built Lochinch Castle, the collections grew in size and complexity, and pictures taken in 1900 show a garden in its major characteristics very similar to that which greets the eye today, though much less dense in growth.

But the story of Castle Kennedy is not yet complete. The 12th earl, who inherited in 1914 when he was a prisoner of war in Germany, proved to be as skilful a gardener as any of his ancestors. From his release in 1918 until his death in 1961 he devoted himself to amassing one of the finest collections of rhododendrons in the British Isles. He found that many of the more tender kinds grew well in the mild, moist climate. The large-leaved species, such as *R. falconeri*, *R. macabeanum* and *R. sino-grande* loved it, and even the fragrant tumpet-flowered *R. lindleyi* from Assam could be grown out of doors. The finest form of this, which received an Award of Merit in 1952, is named 'Lord Stair' and was selected by him at Castle Kennedy.

As a result of his planting the gardens now blaze with colour each spring, reaching a peak in May and early June, when the deciduous azaleas and many of the hybrid rhododendrons are in bloom. Magnolias of many kinds join the earlier rhododendrons together with huge drifts of daffodils, to be followed by scarlet embothriums, planted in Dettingen Avenue with eucryphias and by the canal side with cordylines.

Since the gardens are open to the public daily from April to September, and many visitors enjoy flowers, the 13th earl and his wife, daughter of another famous gardener, the late Sir David Bowes Lyon, have introduced many summer-flowering plants to the old sunken garden beside Lochinch Castle. Here, in what was formerly an elaborate Victorian parterre, they have made a delightfully secluded garden, hemmed in by myrtles, blue gums, Japanese cherries and stocked with ornamental plants of many kinds. It is easy to miss this garden since to reach it one must not merely walk the length of the isthmus but also find the narrow path that leads to it below the main terrace of the house, beside a sunny sheltered border where some of the most tender plants thrive. It is a journey well worth making, for only when it has been completed has the full beauty of these gardens been revealed.

Sheffield Park

Sheffield Park near Uckfield has benefited from two of the great periods in English garden making, the first more than 200 years ago when the landscape movement was at its height and the second between about 1890 and 1920 when plant collecting was in fashion.

Lancelot Brown worked at Sheffield Park, making two of the lakes there and modelling lawns to sweep down to them, with belts and clumps of trees to frame carefully contrived views. Towards the end of the 19th century two more lakes were made by Pulham and Sons of Chelsea for the 3rd Earl of Sheffield and new plants were grouped around them, this time mainly exotic species which found welcome shelter among the native oaks, beeches and Scots pines which had been the chief plant material of 18th-century landscapers. The work of collecting and planting new species gained momentum after Lord Sheffield sold the property to Mr A.G. Soames in 1909 and it still goes on now that the garden, but not the James Wyatt house, belongs to the National Trust.

Now most of these plantings have reached maturity and they fit the landscape so well that it is difficult to remember that they have not always grown there. Great swamp cypresses tower beside the lakes and are splendidly reflected in the water which provides the conditions they require. In drier places incense cedars have formed tall evergreen columns and Brewer's spruce, most beautiful of all weeping conifers, hangs out curtains of dark green leaves. There are probably more specimens of the tupelo tree (*Nyssa sylvatica*) at Sheffield Park than in any other garden in the British Isles.

Hardy palms give the place an almost tropical appearance; rhododendrons, originally planted as individual bushes, have merged into huge evergreen banks; there are scores of Japanese maples, flowering dogwoods and many more lovely things too numerous to catalogue. Sheffield Park has, in fact, become a kind of botanic garden, but with this difference that here the plants are not grouped primarily for scientific purposes but are used with an artist's eye to improve and diversify an already beautiful landscape garden.

Because of its careful planning Sheffield is lovely and composed at all times of the year. It is not dependent on rich colour for this beauty, but there are two seasons of the year when it is ablaze and unquestionably these are the periods when it is most popular with visitors.

The first occurs in spring and early summer, roughly from about mid-April until mid-June. It is then that the rhododendrons and azaleas are at

Overleaf: Autumn at Sheffield Park. The house designed by James Wyatt emerges from the trees in the background

Right: Sheffield Park: exotic trees around the second lake

their peak and the woodlands are carpeted with bluebells. It is a measure of the care that has been taken to create this lovely landscape that the bluebells themselves have been planted. Though they grow naturally in many places nearby (the famous Bluebell railway line has a terminus at Sheffield Park not half a mile from the garden), they did not grow wild in the garden itself and so were introduced in thousands to complete the spring picture.

At this season the cornus bushes are also at their best, white *Cornus kousa*, pink *C. florida rubra* and other kinds and a little earlier there are great drifts of daffodils naturalised in the grass.

The rhododendrons continue late at Sheffield Park for there are hundreds of the old hardy hybrids which were specially bred not to flower before late May so that their blossoms would not be damaged by frost. One of the best hybrids made at Sheffield Park is also late flowering. It is named 'Angelo' and has trusses of huge white, sweetly scented flowers which look much like those of *Rhododendron loderi* but open about a fortnight later.

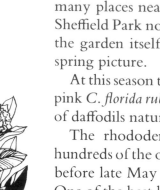

Kalmia latifolia

By the time 'Angelo' is out the kalmias are beginning to bloom and there are a lot of them, not just the fairly well known calico bush, *Kalmia latifolia*, but also the smaller-flowered deeper pink sheep laurel, *K. angustifolia*, which does well in the moist rather heavy soil.

The second season of brilliant colour comes in the autumn, for a great many of the plants at Sheffield Park, particularly around the two upper lakes, have been chosen specifically for this feature. It is then that the delicate foliage of the swamp cypresses turns a vivid cinnamon-red before it falls; the nyssas and azaleas glow with many shades of yellow, orange and crimson and the maples become fiery scarlet. In sharp contrast to these bright colours are the silvery plumes of numerous large clumps of pampas grass and the dusky shades of evergreen conifers.

Those visitors who penetrate a little way into the woods will be rewarded with the spectacle of a great river-like drift of *Gentiana sino-ornata* which is probably the most generous planting of this wonderful azure-flowered Chinese plant to be found anywhere in the British Isles.

It is all these riches that make autumn for me the best of all the seasons at Sheffield Park. Other gardens may rival or even surpass it for spring flowers; few can come near it for autumn colour.

Bodnant

It would, I think, be impossible to discover merely from looking at Bodnant, that this was a garden that had grown over a considerable period of time and not one that had been conceived as a whole from the outset. Today it appears so perfectly integrated with formal features overlooking and leading to progressively informal ones, that it is difficult to imagine that it started as something quite different. Yet so it did and its progress from quite simple beginnings to its present magnificence and variety is one of the great stories of British horticulture.

The gully behind the Pin Mill at Bodnant

It really begins in 1874 when Mr Henry Pochin purchased the property at Tal-y-cafn, Gwynedd though many of the native trees which give it shelter and link it so convincingly with its Snowdonian setting were planted towards the end of the 18th century. To understand what happened it is necessary to have some idea of the nature of the site.

The house stands quite high above the valley of the River Conway on its east side. Though it faces west with views over the valley to the mountains it actually looks down into a narrower and more steeply-sided glen through which the little River Hiraethlyn flows to the Conway. From this a gulley, also serving as a water course, comes up towards the south side of the house, which thus overlooks some very heavily contoured land.

Mr Pochin engaged Mr Milner, a professional landscape architect, to lay out a garden around the house while he proceeded to plant a number of conifers in the glen and elsewhere. When he died in 1895 his daughter, married to the 1st Baron Aberconway, continued to plant the garden but without interfering greatly with the natural contours. By this time two blue Atlas cedars were beginning to dominate the steep slope immediately below the west front.

Though Lady Aberconway was fond of gardening her son, Henry Duncan McLaren, later to become the second baron, was even more enthusiastic and after a few years she entrusted the management of the garden entirely to him. By 1905 he was launched on the architectural project which was to transform Bodnant. He determined to terrace the west slope for about half the distance between house and stream. He drew

all the plans himself making five terraces in all, each different in width, depth, ornamentation and planting but all broadly in what is loosely termed the 'Italian style'. The third and largest of the terraces was designed to accommodate the two cedar trees with a large bow-fronted pool between them and another much longer narrower canal-like pool was constructed on the bottom terrace with a stage and theatre wings cut in yew at its north end. More than thirty years later he was able to purchase in Gloucestershire a very attractive early 18th-century pavilion most of which was removed to Bodnant, restored to perfect condition and erected on new foundations at the southern end of the Canal Terrace, where it completes the picture perfectly. Since, during its period of decline in Gloucestershire, the building had been used for the manufacture of pins it is now known as the Pin Mill.

The gully lies behind the Pin Mill hidden from view by it and the many trees and shrubs planted around the terrace. Here Lord Aberconway made a stream-side rock garden, not for the cultivation of alpines which would have been out of scale as well as out of place, but for more shrubs principally camellias and evergreen azaleas.

While he was engaged in all this new construction he became fascinated by rhododendrons largely, I think, because of regular business engagements in Cornwall which brought him into contact with all the enthusiastic Cornish gardeners, several of whom were busily and successfully hybridising the new Himalayan rhododendron species. Lord Aberconway acquired rhododendrons from Cornwall and elsewhere and was soon producing so many seedlings himself that the garden began to fill up with them. He used numerous species and was successful with many of them but he will always be most remembered by rhododendron growers for the advances he made in red varieties and in particular for his use of *Rhododendron repens* to produce more compact varieties such as 'Elizabeth' named after one of his daughters.

Opposite: The Pin Mill reflected in the canal pool

Right: The laburnum-covered pergola dripping with blossom

The terraces completed, Lord Aberconway turned his attention to the glen where his grandfather's conifers had already grown to considerable size. In the glen there was already an old mill and mill pond. Rhododendrons, azaleas and other shrubs were planted on the slopes of the glen and the stream side was filled with Asiatic primulas, meconopsis and many other herbaceous and shrubby plants. Right below the Canal Terrace he planted the tree magnolias so that it was possible to look down from above at their sumptuous flowers.

The garden grew and grew penetrating even further up the glen and also beyond the lawns on the south side of the house. One of the most admired features here is a circular garden for daphnes surrounded by beds filled with yet more rhododendrons, embothriums and other flowering shrubs. Where the front lawn falls away to the rock garden gulley he made a circular pool and surrounded it entirely with *Rhododendron williamsianum* which is lovely even when out of flower because of its neat, heart-shaped, bronze-tinted leaves.

There are many such felicitous touches at Bodnant and under the care of the 3rd Lord Aberconway and his wife they continue to increase in number. The garden is also constantly growing outwards though now with much less emphasis on rhododendrons and much more on other trees and shrubs, including species and varieties of sorbus, malus and prunus. A great deal has also been done to open new vistas and clear old ones that had become blocked by the luxuriant growth of plants.

Bodnant was presented to the National Trust by the 2nd Baron Aberconway in 1949 but with the condition that he and his heirs should supervise it. So this is yet another garden that has been ensured continuity of purpose and outlook and this has extended even to the head gardener as Mr F.C. Puddle, who came to Bodnant in 1920 was succeeded by his son Charles who remains head gardener to the present day.

Opposite: The water patio of Derwent College, University of York

Stone urns and box-edged beds surround a lawn at Bodnant

The Way Ahead

ne conclusion to be drawn from this short account of garden making in Britain since the days of the Stuart kings is that, though it has often been strongly influenced by architecture and painting, rather more purely horticultural interests have sometimes drawn it into unexpected places. In particular the peculiarly English love of plants, the mildness of the climate and the variety of the soils of the British Isles diverted garden making in these islands from the mainstream of European development. Though that influence has now been greatly modified and brought under control, it is still more powerful here than in any other part of the world.

So what of the future? Will British gardens continue to be dominated for another century by our native pleasure in plants for their own sake or will architecture gain the ascendancy as it has done in America, or have artists some new and significant contribution to make to gardens? Of course, it is impossible to be sure but there are a few viable indications that modern art is making an impact on modern garden design in Britain. There is no evidence of any move towards abstraction, no apparent desire to probe into the inner realities at any rate by amateurs who do by far the largest amount of garden making, which remains traditional, fairly obvious and strongly plant orientated.

The professionals appear to be following a different course and it is one strongly influenced by modern architecture; it is usually functional and occasionally experimental. Landscape architects appear eager to use the new techniques which science and engineering have made available and in large-scale projects, such as those at York University and the Barbican, have produced some interesting results. In both places water features figure prominently and this is true of many smaller gardens. Pools, fountains and cascades have all been made simple to construct by various advances in technology and this could be one of the pointers to the future.

Another could be a greater use of plants selected for their shape and solidity rather than primarily for their texture and colour. There has been a lot of discussion about the so called 'architectural' qualities of some plants such as yuccas and phormiums. Trees are being looked at with increasing interest as individuals, each with a characteristic shape and bearing capable of making a significant contribution to an environment. This is something radically different from the specimen planting of the 19th century when the aim was usually to display the beauty of some tree, often a new or rare kind, rather than to use it specifically as an object, carefully selected and placed in a largely architectural setting.

The development of hedge-cutting machinery has undoubtedly revived interest in the ancient art of topiary and this is being applied in new forms by some modern gardeners. It is one of the features that could be most readily exploited for abstract designs should anyone wish to experiment with them. Added to this, chemicals have been developed which will retard growth or increase the branch density of plants. So far these have been used mainly in a utilitarian way to cut down the cost of pruning fruit trees or to control the growth of trees and shrubs on embankments, but clearly they could have an ornamental application if any landscape designer cared to use them in that way.

In fact the future seems full of promise, with new plants, new machines, new technology and new visions all combining to make possible a new age in garden making.

Opposite: Central Hall, University of York, surrounded by the water garden

University of York

What must be one of the most original landscapes created in Britain this century has been designed as a setting for the new University of York and its nucleus is the 16th-century mansion Heslington Hall on the south-eastern outskirts of York. The hall was built in 1568 by Thomas Eynns (or Eymis), Secretary and Keeper of the Seal to the council set up by Queen Elizabeth for the northern part of England. Legend has it that Eynns built it expressly to lodge the Queen on one of her visits to Yorkshire, but there is nothing to substantiate this. It seems more probable that, like many another fine mansion built in this period, it was intended to establish the social standing of a man who was rising rapidly in wealth and importance.

Heslington Hall is a suitably imposing red-brick building, not unduly ornamented outside but with fine windows, well proportioned, and occupying three sides of a quadrangle open to the east. It was restored and enlarged in 1854, and an earlier picture shows an almost identical main block flanked by considerably simpler wings.

There is no record of garden making at Heslington Hall until a century and a half after it was built. In the intervening years the property had passed first to the Heskeths of Lancashire and then to James Yarborough (or Yarburgh) through his marriage in 1692 to Anne Hesketh, heiress to Thomas Hesketh. He it was, we are told, who planted the avenue of yew trees on the terrace to the west of the house, and he too must almost certainly have built the tall brick pavilion that stands at the north-eastern corner of the terrace, where it commands good views of the house, terrace and park, as well as overlooking the high wall that separates the pleasure garden from the kitchen garden. A painting dated 1760 shows house and garden much as James and Ann must have planned it and also reveals that in those days a little formal canal was centred on the pavilion and extended from it into the park at right angles to the terrace and yew avenue. It is all very neat and formal and the yew trees, though 400 years old, remain remarkably slender and separate.

This is a scene very different from that which existed in 1900, when Heslington Hall and its garden were first described and illustrated in *Country Life*, and the writer could compare the huge clipped yews with the more publicised topiary of Levens Hall, though conceding that those at Heslington were less elaborately shaped. The canal, too had disappeared, to be replaced by a small ham-shaped lake or fish pond a little farther from the terrace, in the middle distance of the view from house to park.

Though in itself a modest landscape feature in a by then thoroughly conventional style, this little lake is of importance since it suggested the main feature of the new landscape that was to be created for the University of York. Most of the extra land required for this lies to the west of the hall and is flat, but to the north-west it rises steeply some 70 feet to Heslington Hill, where once Cromwell's troops were bombarded by Royalists from the beleaguered walls of York. No doubt it was to drain the low-lying garden of Heslington Hall that the 18th-century canal and 19th-century fish pool were constructed; and what could be more sensible than to continue with the same idea but magnified to meet the scale of the new development. A vast waterscape has therefore been created by extending the little fish pool for nearly a mile, almost to the south-west corner of the site, but giving it form and interest by making it wind through the flat land like a river and using the spoil to provide some new and pleasing contours. By this means drainage problems have been solved in an economical way and a design created that is both novel and highly effective.

Maintenance costs are also relatively low since water, unlike lawns and flower borders, needs no mowing or cultivation. Photographs taken after the construction of this great water feature, but before any building was begun, show that it was in its own right a highly successful treatment of the landscape. Since many of the new buildings are exciting in shape and well placed to exploit the reflective qualities of the water in the most dramatic fashion, the overall effect now that the development approaches completion commands admiration.

In addition to its beauty, there are several points of special technical interest that merit attention. Though the volume of water in this 15-acre lake is immense (its average depth is between 3 and 4 feet and it contains something like 14 million gallons of water), it is retained by a remarkably small and slim dam. This is possible because at its south-western end the artificial 'river' develops into a broad bow containing a lozenge-shaped island and then rapidly narrows, taking an opposite bend to reach the dam. The result is that if the slow flow of water down the 'river' is accelerated by strong winds from the north or east the surge is largely absorbed in the bow and further dampened by the island so that no undue pressure ever reaches the dam.

Vast waterscape surrounded by college buildings

University of York: a Henry Moore group links the old topiary garden of Heslington Hall with the new university campus. This group has now been replaced with another by the same sculptor

A second point is that for speed and economy in construction the entire area was lined with black polythene delivered in sheets, each about one acre in extent, to be lapped and welded on site. These gigantic sheets were bedded on sand and covered with coarse gravel and sand. This method of construction has proved entirely successful, and though the sheet is now ruptured in places, the soil has meantime become sufficiently consolidated by the weight of water to be reasonably impervious.

The pillars of bridges crossing the water at several different points have also tapped spring water, and this, bringing up minerals from below, has proved beneficial to the fish with which the lake has been stocked. Over 8,000 fish were introduced during the past six years, including carp, tench, rudd, golden orfe, rainbow trout and brown trout. Some sections are reserved for fishing, one for swimming and the widest central area for boating and sailing. Here there is a powerful single-jet fountain that, like so much else at York University, serves a dual role, part aesthetic, part utilitarian, for in addition to making a striking plume of water, which on a windy day can drift right across the lake, it also helps to aerate the water, to the great benefit of the fish.

The whole new water feature has been linked to Heslington Hall in an ingenious way. A section of the old topiary garden near the house has been cleared and a long canal pool with a line of low-spraying fountains has been constructed across it. This leads the eye to the nearest of the new buildings, Derwent College, a short distance to the north, built in part around a rectangular pool with several lines of fountains similar to those on the terrace. These can be seen through the pillars of a covered walk around the pool, and from within this water patio there is a similar outward view to the west to the enlarged fish pond into which its overflow cascades. There is, in consequence, an immediate connection between the old garden and the new, and a logical progression from a formal to an informal style. A Henry Moore sculpture placed among the yew trees overlooking the canal pool completes the link between old and new and sits perfectly in this setting.

Further changes of mood are revealed as the water garden is further explored. The fish pond is generously furnished with marginal plants and stocked with wildfowl, but beyond it the water narrows almost to a stream, the banks are grassy and the area is reserved for fishing. Then it widens to enter the central basin, which might suggest a harbour since there are large paved areas with bollards placed as if for use as moorings and wide flights of steps leading down to the water's edge.

Some of the most striking buildings are placed around this basin. To the east is the bulging, irregularly hexagonal shape of Central Hall surmounted by spare roof stays projecting skywards like some strange derrick. To the north is Vanbrugh College with its rows of conical top lights and the largest and most elaborately patterned of all the paved areas. The extensive physics laboratories are to the south, the lecture hall jutting out over the water like an overhanging cliff with large square stepping stones in the water beneath as a pedestrian short cut to Goodricke College to the west. This is simple in construction, but lights from the building play down on to the water and nearby there is a sandy beach for swimmers. A long covered bridge crosses the water to rejoin Vanbrugh College and also lead to the biology laboratory to the west, where the water once more resumes a river-like course and flows between meadows that, to turn them into a bird sanctuary, have been fenced against foxes.

To make way for all this development some mature trees had to be felled and others severely lopped, but from 1964 onwards new planting has been undertaken on a large scale, something like four to five thousand trees and shrubs being added every year. Much of the tree planting is in belts running from the lower to the higher land, so that they give maximum protection from the north east and the south west and also emphasise the natural contours of the land. Smaller trees are used as specimens in the many areas of mown grass, and shrubs to give definition and fill in space where this is necessary.

When James Yarborough lived at Heslington Hall in the early 18th century his daughter married John Vanbrugh, who was building Castle Howard for Lord Carlisle, some 14 miles away. Many of the trees for the new university campus have come from Castle Howard, and with the aid of a Newman transplanter it is possible to bring in specimens 30 feet and more in height with little difficulty or damage – a technical feat that Carlisle would surely have admired. I think that however strange he might find the new buildings he would also approve the boldness of the new landscape garden – a very English style of which he was one of the originators.

The Barbican

When, soon after the war, it was decided to redevelop the whole bombed-out area around the Barbican in an imaginative way to provide for a composite community of office workers, residents and students plus an arts centre, it was clear that the open spaces left between and around the new and old buildings were going to be as important as the buildings themselves. They would have to provide an appropriate setting for structures of many kinds and at the same time serve the amenity requirements of the large number of people who would be using the area, some more or less permanently, some fairly regularly especially on weekdays and some more casually as shoppers or visitors to the various exhibitions, concerts and theatrical performances that would be a feature of the new Barbican life.

There were, however, serious difficulties to be overcome. First, part of the site was over the Metropolitan and Circle underground railways and it was a feature of the plan to further undermine it with subterranean garages and all the services essential for a large community. So over a considerable area there would be no natural soil and no chance of bringing imported soil and placing it in contact with a natural subsoil which could serve as a water reservoir for it and also provide it with drainage.

Another problem was that amongst the new buildings, all of which were to be highly modern in design and would include some skyscrapers, there would remain a few very old structures which had either miraculously survived the bombing or had been revealed by it in the course of subsequent excavation and clearance. These included St Giles Church, a part of the old wall that had encircled London in Roman times and the bastions of what was believed to be a mediaeval wall. Professor Grimes, an archaeologist working for the City of London, was anxious that a berm, the old name for the ledge between the base of a fortification and its ditch, should be constructed between these ancient remains and a canal which flowed beside them.

All these considerations pointed in a similar direction, towards the construction of a water garden in which the requirements for soil and plants would be reduced to a minimum. The idea first began to surface in 1953 and by 1959 designs prepared by the architects Chamberlain, Powell and Bon had been approved by the City of London but for various reasons construction did not begin until 1971. At the time of writing it is still not complete and is unlikely to be so before 1980 at earliest. Yet enough has been done to give a clear idea of what the final effect will be.

There are already two large rectangular sheets of water at different levels linked by a wide cascade or weir. From the Lower Lake a canal wraps around what looks rather like a jetty on which stand St Giles Church and the assembly hall of the City of London School of Girls linking with the canal and berm beside the ancient walls and fortifications.

The Upper Lake is enclosed on three sides by high residential buildings, the cascade actually being beneath the block which fills the western side. On the fourth northerly side is a lawn with a pergola and some scattered

Concrete cascade and waterfall in the Barbican water garden

trees and beyond that a new music rehearsal room. Water flows into this lake at its eastern end by way of a highly formalised waterfall with completely undisguised concrete. It is possible to walk beneath this and view the lake and buildings through a curtain of falling water and there are pools and inlets filled with a profusion of aquatic plants with more moisture-loving kinds in the damp soil around.

At the west end of the lake is a group of seven circular 'islands' constructed of concrete and brick and completely formalised like the cascade and waterfall. One can walk out on to them by a causeway and sit in them with the water lapping at one's side. The islands are arranged like the segments of a pinnate leaf, a rose leaf let us suppose, and are covered with canopies of light iron work on which it was intended to train wisterias. Like some of the other planting in this highly imaginative garden this went wrong at the outset, the planners having failed to make the troughs that were to contain the roots sufficiently large for the hungry wisterias. But the idea is admirable and the technical fault can be easily overcome by choosing some less demanding climbers such as vines.

The Lower Lake is far more open with St Giles Church to the south and paved terraces rising in shallow steps to the concert hall and theatre still under construction to the north. When this is complete thirty-three fountains arranged in three rows of eleven, will play in the lake itself and five more fountains will throw their water into five large circular basins on the terraces. It is typical of the functional thinking behind so much modern professional landscaping that the lake fountains will serve a dual purpose, part utilitarian, part aesthetic since they will be fed by the cooling water from the Arts Centre air-conditioning system. The very novelty of this idea has brought about delays in its execution since it is estimated that the fountains will raise the temperature of the Lower Lake by two or three degrees and fears have been expressed that this may be bad for the fish with which the lake will be stocked, since it will lower the level of dissolved oxygen, and that it will also encourage the growth of algae. However, the scheme is to go ahead and time will prove whether these fears are justified.

Opposite: Circular islands for relaxation in the Upper Lake of the Barbican
Right: The Barbican: a water curtain falls from beneath the cascade

Though planting around the water garden has been kept to a minimum some of it is quite ambitious. For example in St Giles Square, the name given to the area around the old chancel, quite a lot of magnolias are growing including the magnificent but slow-maturing *Magnolia camp-bellii*, several good forms of *M. soulangeana* and the much less familiar, small-flowered but very prolific *M. kobus*. The cricket-bat willow also grows well and looks entirely right by the water.

To the west of the Lower Lake is one of the few areas where there are no obstacles below ground, no garages, underground railways or even sewers. Here surface soil can actually be in contact with subsoil and the normal interchanges of moisture can take place. It is not surprising that here are the best lawns and the finest trees including limes and willows. Even rhododendrons thrive as they do in Parliament Square, though there they are used like bedding plants to be removed and grown elsewhere when they are not in flower. In the more permanent planting of the Barbican it might be preferable to stick to shrubs and trees that are less dependant on flowers for beauty.

However this is a tiny criticism when considered against the imaginative success of the whole scheme. Another fault is a little more serious. It concerns the management of the small terrace gardens which jut out toward Fore Street on the southern side of Andrews House like a row of great concrete wheelbarrows. Architecturally they seem rather ugly but that would scarcely be noticed were they well-filled with suitable plants. In reality each has been left to be planted and tended by the owner of the flat which it adjoins. The result is a rather hideous patchwork of styles ranging from just acceptable to complete neglect. Since every passer-by on the raised walkways, which are an essential feature of the whole Barbican development and which provide such magnificent platforms for viewing buildings and gardens, must look down on this example of bad gardening it would seem better to take it out of the hands of amateurs and entrust it to the City of London professionals.

42

• Inverness 41

40
Aberdeen •

39

38   37
35

Glasgow •   36
•   Edinburgh
34

32

33

Belfast
43

31
30
29

Dublin •   Liverpool •
28
44   25   26   27
                                        24   21
Limerick •   22

47   23   Birmingham •
46
45   20

                                                      19

                                    Cardiff •
                                            17   18
Cork •   London
                                                    4 3 2   1
                                              16   5 6
                                         15   10 9 7
                                                            8
                                12 • Exeter   11
                           13

Scilly Isles °₀14

1 *The Barbican*
City of London

2 *Waterhouse Plantation*
Bushy Park, Hampton, Middlesex

3 *Isabella Plantation*
Richmond Park, Richmond, Surrey

4 *Savill Garden and Valley Gardens*
Windsor Great Park, Englefield Green, Berkshire

5 *Hever Castle*
Edenbridge, Kent

6 *Sissinghurst Castle*
Sissinghurst, Kent

7 *Scotney Castle*
Lamberhurst, Kent

8 *Sheffield Park Gardens*
nr. Uckfield, East Sussex

9 *Leonardslee*
Horsham, West Sussex

10 *Nymans*
Handcross, West Sussex

11 *Cranbourne Manor*
Cranbourne, Wimborne, Dorset

12 *Killerton*
nr. Exeter, Devon

13 *Lanhydrock Park*
nr. Bodmin, Cornwall

14 *Tresco Abbey*
Tresco, Isles of Scilly

15 *Hestercombe*
nr. Taunton, Somerset

16 *Stourhead*
Stourton, nr. Mere, Wiltshire

27 *Westonbirt Arboretum*
Westonbirt, Tetbury, Gloucestershire

18 *Ascott*
Wing, Buckinghamshire

19 *Hidcote Manor*
Hidcote Bartrim, nr. Chipping Camden, Gloucestershire

20 *Burford House*
Tenbury Wells, Worcestershire

21 *Alton Towers*
Cheadle, Staffordshire

22 *Powis Castle*
Welshpool, Powys, Wales

23 *The University College of Wales*
Aberystwyth, Dyfed, Wales

24 *Portmeirion*
Gwynedd, Wales

25 *Bodnant*
Tal-y-Cafn, Gwynedd, Wales

26 *Arley Hall*
Northwich, Cheshire

27 *Chatsworth*
Bakewell, Derbyshire

28 *Bramham Park*
Wetherby, Boston Spa, West Yorkshire

29 *University of York*
Heslington, York

30 *Sutton Park*
Sutton-on-the-Forest, North Yorkshire

31 *Studley Royal and Fountains Abbey*
Studley Roger, nr. Ripon, North Yorkshire

32 *Wallington*
Cambo, Northumberland

33 *Castle Kennedy and Lochinch*
Stranraer, Dumfries and Galloway Region, Scotland

34 *Achamore House*
Isel of Gigha, Strathclyde Region, Scotland

35 *The Younger Botanic Gardens*
Benmore, Strathclyde Region, Scotland

36 *Tyninghame*
Tyninghame, Lothian, Scotland

37 *Falkland Palace*
Fife, Fife Region, Scotland

38 *Drummond Castle*
Crieff, Tayside Region, Scotland

39 *Edzell Castle*
Edzell, Brechin, Tayside Region, Scotland

40 *Crathes Castle*
Banchory, Grampian Region, Scotland

41 *Pitmedden*
Pitmedden, Udney, Grampian Region, Scotland

42 *Inverewe*
Poolewe, Highland Region, Scotland

43 *Mount Stewart*
Co. Down, Northern Ireland

44 *Tully House*
Kildare, Co. Kildare, Republic of Ireland

45 *Garinish Island*
Co. Cork, Republic of Ireland

46 *Derreen*
Lauragh, Co. Kerry, Republic of Ireland

47 *Rossdohan Island*
nr. Parknasilla, Co. Kerry, Republic of Ireland

Glossary

ALLÉE An enclosed walk usually between closely planted trees or shrubs. Since the 16th-century French gardeners have made great use of allées; crossing to make complex patterns or radiating like the ribs of a fan

ARBORETUM A collection of trees usually including exotic and unusual kinds of scientific interest

ARCHER, THOMAS An architect who lived from 1608 to 1743 and favoured the baroque style. He designed numerous pavilions and other ornamental buildings for gardens

AUGUSTA, PRINCESS Wife of Frederick, Prince of Wales and eldest son of George II, and mother of George III. She was keenly interested in plants, spent much of her time living at Kew House and made many improvements to the garden there. She laid the foundation of the Kew botanical collection

BALUSTRADE A row of short pillars surmounted by a top rail or coping

BARRY, SIR CHARLES An architect who lived from 1795 to 1860. He designed the Houses of Parliament and many country houses and also terraces for some famous gardens

BELVEDERE A turret or look out designed to command a view of special beauty

BONSAI Artificially dwarfed trees. The word is Japanese

BOSCAGE Alternatively spelled 'boskage'. A dense planting of trees often used as the infilling between allées

BROWN, LANCELOT Gardener and garden designer who lived from 1716 to 1783. He was born at Kirkharle, Northumberland, worked at Stowe under William Kent for Lord Cobham and, in 1751, launched out on his own as a garden designer in the new landscape style. He also designed some country houses. He acquired the nickname 'Capability' from the frequency with which he assured potential clients that their estates afforded great capability for improvement

BRIDGEMAN, CHARLES A garden designer who died in 1738. He worked at a time when the old formal gardens were being replaced by the new landscape gardens and his style evolved with this change. Towards the end of his life he collaborated with William Kent who was much more directly involved in the introduction of landscape gardening

CHEERE, JOHN An 18th-century maker of garden ornaments, many cast in lead. He took over from John Van Nost and probably continued to use many of his moulds

EYE CATCHER Any building, ornament, statue or other object placed specifically to attract attention. Eye catchers were much used by 18th-century landscape designers as focal points in the most important views or vistas

FLITCROFT, HENRY An architect who lived from 1697 to 1769. He was a protegé of Lord Burlington and was later employed by the Board of Works. He designed ornamental buildings for several famous gardens

FOWLER, CHARLES An architect who lived from 1781 to 1867. He designed part of Covent Garden market and the Old Harringay market and also the curving conservatory with central dome at Syon House

FOLLY Literally a costly and useless building, but in fact follies often contribute some element to the design of a garden that seems essential to its creator

GAZEBO A structure designed to command a view. However the term is usually applied to garden pavilions, most commonly those that have two stories

GNOMON That part of a sundial which casts the shadow indicating the time

GROTTO A cave or cave-like structure often decorated inside with shells, fossils, stones and other natural objects

HA-HA A sunken wall and ditch originally used in fortifications but taken over by garden designers as a means of keeping out cattle and yet creating, from the garden, an illusion that it extended without a break into the surrounding countryside

HUSSEY, CHRISTOPHER EDWARD CLIVE Writer on the country houses of Britain who lived from 1899 to 1970. He was at one time editor of Country Life magazine and contributed many articles. He also wrote several books, including 'The Picturesque', 'English Gardens and Landscapes 1700–1750' and 'The Life of Sir Edwin Lutyens'. He lived at Scotney Castle where he preserved and improved the picturesque landscape created by his grandfather, Edward Hussey

KENNEDY, GEORGE Little seems to be known about this man except that he designed terraces for Bowood in 1841 and that he prepared a plan of the great parterre at Drummond Castle, though whether this was for a revision of the design or merely a record of what was already there is not clear. He may have been a son of Louis Kennedy who was factor at Drummond Castle

KNOT A pattern formed with small clipped shrubs, usually box but occasionally lavender or thyme. Knots were fashionable in the 16th and 17th centuries and the patterns were often elaborate and cunningly devised to produce the 'under and over' effect of embroidery

LOGGIA Literally an open gallery but the term is often used for any open-sided garden room or shelter

LONDON AND WISE George London, who died in 1713 and Henry Wise, who died in 1738, were partners in the Brompton Park Nursery, Kensington. This nursery reached the height of its fame during their time of ownership and provided plants for many of the most famous gardens of the period. London also worked as a garden designer, following the formal style of the 17th century

LORRAINE, CLAUDE A French painter who lived from 1600 to 1682 and spent much of his time in Rome. The mythical and historical subjects in which he specialised were remarkable for the carefully composed landscapes in which they were set. It was these pictures which provided some of the inspiration of the landscape style which revolutionised English garden making during the 18th century. His real name was Claude Gelée and he was born in Lorraine

MOUNT An artificial mound or bank made in the garden as a vantage point from which to view the garden and the surrounding country. Mounts were a feature of many early gardens

NESFIELD, WILLIAM ANDREWS A military engineer who became an artist and garden designer. He lived from 1793 to 1864 and played a notable part in the creation of terraces and parterres in gardens during the mid-19th century

OBELISK A tapering shaft of masonry usually rectalinear in section. Obelisks were at one time much favoured as eye catchers or focal points in man-made landscapes

ORANGERY The first plant houses were made primarily to protect orange bushes in winter. In consequence these houses were known as orangeries though they often contained other plants as well

PAGODA Chinese or Indian buildings usually tall, slender and slightly tapering, surmounted by a peaked roof and often with several more roofs at lower levels, one for each storey of the building. They were originally intended for religious purposes but were copied by British garden makers for purely ornamental purposes

PALLADIO, ANDREA An Italian architect who lived from 1518 to 1580. He formulated what he believed to be the classical proportions for building. Many ornamental structures in 18th-century gardens were based on these principles

PARTERRE A level area in a garden, usually divided to form a symmetrical pattern and often with matching flower beds or scroll work cut in small evergreen shrubs such as box, though parterres can be of any degree of elaboration or simplicity

PEARCE, GEORGE A. An architect working for the Ministry of Building and Works and seconded by the Ministry to design new exhibition plant houses for the Royal Botanic Garden, Edinburgh. These broke new structural ground by being almost entirely suspended from outside by steel cables and gantries so that very large panes of glass could be used and all interior pillars eliminated. He later designed a smaller greenhouse on the same lines for the Duke of Devonshire at Chatsworth

PEDIMENT The broadly triangular structure used by Greek builders to cap the portico or columned entrance to a building. The style was much copied during the classical revival of the 18th century and is characteristic of many Georgian buildings

PERGOLA A walk covered with plants usually trained over a framework of pillars and cross members

PINETUM A collection of mainly coniferous trees usually containing kinds that are rare or of scientific interest

PORTICO A roof supported on columns. Porticos were used by Greek and Roman builders and were copied by British architects when these classical styles became fashionable in the 17th and 18th centuries

PUGIN, AUGUSTUS WELBY NORTHMORE An architect who lived from 1812 to 1852 and was much involved in the revival of interest in the gothic style

REPTON, HUMPHRY An artist who lived from 1752 to 1815 and became one of the most fashionable and influential garden designers after the death of Lancelot Brown in 1783. He restored formality to gardens around the house and helped to bring flowering plants back into the mainstream of garden making

ROBINSON, WILLIAM A gardener who became a writer and editor of gardening books and magazines. He lived from 1839 to 1935, liked the hardy perennial plants of the Northern Hemisphere, favoured what he regarded as more natural styles of garden design and exercised a great influence over the garden thoughts of his times

ROSA, SALVATOR Another of the 17th-century artists working in Italy who, like Claude Lorraine, inspired many garden makers in England during the following century to emulate the landscape he painted. He lived from 1615 to 1673 and worked in a style much more romantic and wild than that of either Claude Lorraine or Gaspar Poussin (1613 to 1675) a third Italian-based artist whose landscapes were much admired by Englishmen

RUSSELL, JAMES A contemporary garden designer born in 1920 and particularly concerned with gardens made largely with plants, many of them exotic. At one time he owned the Sunningdale Nursery

TOPIARY Shrubs clipped into artificial shapes

TUFA A very porous type of sandstone which, because of its sponge-like texture, can hold a lot of water and support plants grown on it with little or no soil

VAN NOST, JOHN A maker of garden ornaments, urns and statues cast in lead. He worked in London during the late 17th and early 18th centuries and eventually sold his yard and moulds to John Cheere

VISTA A view framed in trees or other plants

WILDERNESS Literally a part of the garden allowed to grow as if uncultivated. However the term was much used by early garden makers for areas densely planted with trees or shrubs intersected by a maze-like system of paths

WYATT, JAMES An architect who lived from 1746 to 1813. His style was romantic or neo-gothic and at one time he was Surveyor General to the Board of Trade

Index